White Fragility

ROBIN DIANGELO

White Fragility

*Why It's So Hard for White
People to Talk About Racism*

ALLEN LANE
an imprint of
PENGUIN BOOKS

ALLEN LANE

UK | USA | Canada | Ireland | Australia
India | New Zealand | South Africa

Penguin Books is part of the Penguin Random House group of companies
whose addresses can be found at global.penguinrandomhouse.com.

First published in the United States of America by Beacon Press 2018
First published in Great Britain by Allen Lane 2019

009

Copyright © Robin DiAngelo, 2018

The moral right of the author has been asserted

Printed and bound in Great Britain by Clays Ltd, Elcograf S.p.A.

A CIP catalogue record for this book is available from the British Library

ISBN: 978–0–141–99056–9

www.greenpenguin.co.uk

MIX
Paper from
responsible sources
FSC® C018179

Penguin Random House is committed to a
sustainable future for our business, our readers
and our planet. This book is made from Forest
Stewardship Council® certified paper.

*These ceremonials in honor of white supremacy,
performed from babyhood, slip from the
conscious mind down deep into muscles . . .
and become difficult to tear out.*

—LILLIAN SMITH, *Killers of the Dream* (1949)

CONTENTS

AUTHOR'S NOTE

IDENTITY POLITICS

The United States was founded on the principle that all people are created equal. Yet the nation began with the attempted genocide of Indigenous people and the theft of their land. American wealth was built on the labor of kidnapped and enslaved Africans and their descendants. Women were denied the right to vote until 1920, and black women were denied access to that right until 1964. The term *identity politics* refers to the focus on the barriers specific groups face in their struggle for equality. We have yet to achieve our founding principle, but any gains we have made thus far have come through identity politics.

The identities of those sitting at the tables of power in this country have remained remarkably similar: white, male, middle- and upper-class, able-bodied. Acknowledging this fact may be dismissed as political correctness, but it is still a fact. The decisions made at those tables affect the lives of those not at the tables. Exclusion by those at the table doesn't depend on willful intent; we don't have to intend to exclude for the results of our actions to be exclusion. While implicit bias is always at play because all humans have bias, inequity can occur simply through homogeneity; if I am not aware of the barriers you face, then I won't see them, much less be motivated to remove them. Nor will I be motivated to remove the barriers if they provide an advantage to which I feel entitled.

All progress we have made in the realm of civil rights has been accomplished through identity politics: women's suffrage, the American with Disabilities Act, Title 9, federal recognition of same-sex marriage. A key issue in the 2016 presidential election was the white working class. These are all manifestations of identity politics.

Take women's suffrage. If being a woman denies you the right to vote, you ipso facto cannot grant it to yourself. And you certainly cannot vote for your right to vote. If men control all the mechanisms that exclude women from voting as well as the mechanisms that can reverse that exclusion, women must call on men for justice. You could not have had a conversation about women's right to vote and men's need to grant it without naming women and men. Not naming the groups that face barriers only serves those who already have access; the assumption is that the access enjoyed by the controlling group is universal. For example, although we are taught that women were granted suffrage in 1920, we ignore the fact that it was white women who received full access or that it was white men who granted it. Not until the 1960s, through the Voting Rights Act, were all women—regardless of race—granted full access to suffrage. Naming who has access and who doesn't guides our efforts in challenging injustice.

This book is unapologetically rooted in identity politics. I am white and am addressing a common white dynamic. I am mainly writing to a white audience; when I use the terms *us* and *we*, I am referring to the white collective. This usage may be jarring to white readers because we are so rarely asked to think about ourselves or fellow whites in racial terms. But rather than retreat in the face of that discomfort, we can practice building our stamina for the critical examination of white identity—a necessary antidote to white fragility. This raises another issue rooted in identity politics: in speaking as a white person to a primarily white audience, I am yet again centering white people and the white voice. I have not found a way around this dilemma, for as an insider I can speak to the white experience in ways that may be harder to deny. So, though I am centering the white voice, I am also using my insider status to challenge racism. To not use my position this way is to uphold racism, and that is unacceptable; it is a "both/and" that I must live with. I would never suggest that mine is the only voice that should be heard, only that it is one of the many pieces needed to solve the overall puzzle.

People who do not identify as white may also find this book helpful for understanding why it is so often difficult to talk to white people about racism. People of color cannot avoid understanding white consciousness to some degree if they are to be successful in this society, yet nothing in dominant culture affirms their understanding or validates their frustrations when they interact with white people. I hope that this exploration affirms the cross-racial experiences of people of color and provides some useful insight.

This book looks at the United States and the general context of the West (United States, Canada, and Europe). It does not address nuances and variations within other sociopolitical settings. However, these patterns have also been observed in white people in other white settler societies such as Australia, New Zealand, and South Africa.

WHAT ABOUT MULTIRACIAL PEOPLE?

Throughout this book, I argue that racism is deeply complex and nuanced, and given this, we can never consider our learning to be complete or finished. One example of this complexity is in the very use of the racial categories "white" and "people of color." I use the terms *white* and *people of color* to indicate the two macro-level, socially recognized divisions of the racial hierarchy. Yet in using these terms, I am collapsing a great deal of variation. And though I believe (for reasons explained in chapter 1) that temporarily suspending individuality to focus on group identity is healthy for white people, doing so has very different impacts on people of color. For multiracial people in particular, these binary categories leave them in a frustrating "middle."

Multiracial people, because they challenge racial constructs and boundaries, face unique challenges in a society in which racial categories have profound meaning. The dominant society will assign them the racial identity they most physically resemble, but their own internal racial identity may not align with the assigned identity. For example, though the musician Bob Marley was multiracial, society perceived him as black and thus responded to him as if he were black. When multiracial people's racial identity is ambiguous, they will face constant pressure to explain themselves and "choose a side." Racial identity for multiracial people is further complicated by the racial identity of their parents and the racial demographics of the community in which they are raised. For example, though a child may look black and be treated as black, she may be raised primarily by a white parent and thus identify more strongly as white.

The dynamics of what is termed "passing"—being perceived as white—will also shape a multiracial person's identity, as passing will grant him or her society's rewards of whiteness. However, people of mixed racial heritage who pass as white may also experience resentment and isolation from people of color who cannot pass. Multiracial people may not be seen as "real" people of color or "real" whites. (It is worth noting that though the term "passing" refers to the ability to blend in as a white person, there is no corresponding term for the ability to pass as a person of color. This highlights the fact that, in a racist society, the desired direction is always toward whiteness and away from being perceived as a person of color.)

I will not be able to do justice to the complexity of multiracial identity. But for the purposes of grappling with white fragility, I offer multiracial people the concept of *saliency*. We all occupy multiple and intersecting social positionalities. I am white, but I am also a cisgender woman, able-bodied, and middle-aged. These identities don't cancel out one another; each is more or less salient in different contexts. For example, in a group in which I am the only woman, gender will likely be very salient for me. When I am in a group that is all white except for one person of color, race will likely be my most salient identity. As you read, it will be for you to decide what speaks to your experience and what doesn't, and in what contexts. My hope is that you may gain insight into why people who identify as white are so difficult in conversations regarding race and/or gain insight into your own racial responses as you navigate the roiling racial waters of daily life.

White Fragility

WE CAN'T GET
THERE FROM HERE

*I am a white woman. I am standing beside a black woman. We
are facing a group of white people seated in front of us. We are
in their workplace and have been hired by their employer to lead
them in a dialogue about race. The room is filled with tension and
charged with hostility. I have just presented a definition of racism
that includes the acknowledgment that whites hold social and institutional power over people of color. A white man is pounding
his fist on the table. As he pounds, he yells, "A white person can't
get a job anymore!" I look around the room and see forty employees, thirty-eight of whom are white. Why is this white man so
angry? Why is he being so careless about the impact of his anger?
Why doesn't he notice the effect this outburst is having on the few
people of color in the room? Why are all the other white people
either sitting in silent agreement with him or tuning out? I have,
after all, only articulated a definition of racism.*

White people in North America live in a society that is deeply separate
and unequal by race, and white people are the beneficiaries of that separation and inequality. As a result, we are insulated from racial stress, at
the same time that we come to feel entitled to and deserving of our advantage. Given how seldom we experience racial discomfort in a society

we dominate, we haven't had to build our racial stamina. Socialized into a deeply internalized sense of superiority that we either are unaware of or can never admit to ourselves, we become highly fragile in conversations about race. We consider a challenge to our racial worldviews as a challenge to our very identities as good, moral people. Thus, we perceive any attempt to connect us to the system of racism as an unsettling and unfair moral offense. The smallest amount of racial stress is intolerable—the mere suggestion that being white has meaning often triggers a range of defensive responses. These include emotions such as anger, fear, and guilt and behaviors such as argumentation, silence, and withdrawal from the stress-inducing situation. These responses work to reinstate white equilibrium as they repel the challenge, return our racial comfort, and maintain our dominance within the racial hierarchy. I conceptualize this process as *white fragility*. Though white fragility is triggered by discomfort and anxiety, it is born of superiority and entitlement. White fragility is not weakness per se. In fact, it is a powerful means of white racial control and the protection of white advantage.

Summarizing the familiar patterns of white people's responses to racial discomfort as white fragility has resonated for many people. The sensibility is so familiar because whereas our personal narratives vary, we are all swimming in the same racial water. For me, the recognition has come through my work. I have a rare job; on a daily basis I lead primarily white audiences in discussions of race, something many of us avoid at all costs.

In the early days of my work as what was then termed a diversity trainer, I was taken aback by how angry and defensive so many white people became at the suggestion that they were connected to racism in any way. The very idea that they would be required to attend a workshop on racism outraged them. They entered the room angry and made that feeling clear to us throughout the day as they slammed their notebooks down on the table, refused to participate in exercises, and argued against any and all points.

I couldn't understand their resentment or disinterest in learning more about such a complex social dynamic as racism. These reactions were especially perplexing when there were few or no people of color in their workplace, and they had the opportunity to learn from my cofacilitators of color. I assumed that in these circumstances, an educational workshop on racism would be appreciated. After all, didn't the lack of diversity indicate a problem or at least suggest that some perspectives were missing? Or that the participants might be undereducated about race because of scant cross-racial interactions?

It took me several years to see beneath these reactions. At first I was intimidated by them, and they held me back and kept me careful and quiet. But over time, I began to see what lay beneath this anger and resistance to discuss race or listen to people of color. I observed consistent responses from a variety of participants. For example, many white participants who lived in white suburban neighborhoods and had no sustained relationships with people of color were absolutely certain that they held no racial prejudice or animosity. Other participants simplistically reduced racism to a matter of nice people versus mean people. Most appeared to believe that racism ended in 1865 with the end of slavery. There was both knee-jerk defensiveness about any suggestion that being white had meaning and a refusal to acknowledge any advantage to being white. Many participants claimed white people were now the oppressed group, and they deeply resented anything perceived to be a form of affirmative action. These responses were so predictable—so consistent and reliable—I was able to stop taking the resistance personally, get past my own conflict avoidance, and reflect on what was behind them.

I began to see what I think of as the pillars of whiteness—the unexamined beliefs that prop up our racial responses. I could see the power of the belief that only bad people were racist, as well as how individualism allowed white people to exempt themselves from the forces of socialization. I could see how we are taught to think about racism only as discrete acts committed by individual people, rather than as a complex, interconnected system. And in light of so many white expressions of resentment toward people of color, I realized that we see ourselves as entitled to, and deserving of, more than people of color deserve; I saw our investment in a system that serves us. I also saw how hard we worked to deny all this and how defensive we became when these dynamics were named. In turn, I saw how our defensiveness maintained the racial status quo.

Personal reflections on my own racism, a more critical view of media and other aspects of culture, and exposure to the perspectives of many brilliant and patient mentors of color all helped me to see how these pillars of racism worked. It became clear that if I believed that only bad people who intended to hurt others because of race could ever do so, I would respond with outrage to any suggestion that I was involved in racism. Of course that belief would make me feel falsely accused of something terrible, and of course I would want to defend my character (and I had certainly had many of my own moments of responding in just those ways to reflect on). I came to see that the way we are taught to define racism makes it virtually impossible for white people to understand it. Given our racial insulation, coupled with misinformation, any suggestion that we are complicit in racism is a kind of unwelcome and insulting shock to the system.

If, however, I understand racism as a system into which I was socialized, I can receive feedback on my problematic racial patterns as a helpful way to support my learning and growth. One of the greatest social fears for a white person is being told that something that we have said or done is racially problematic. Yet when someone lets us know that we have just done such a thing, rather than respond with gratitude and relief (after all, now that we are informed, we won't do it again), we often respond with anger and denial. Such moments can be experienced as something valuable, even if temporarily painful, only after we accept that racism is unavoidable and that it is impossible to completely escape having developed problematic racial assumptions and behaviors.

None of the white people whose actions I describe in this book would identify as racist. In fact, they would most likely identify as racially progressive and vehemently deny any complicity with racism. Yet all their responses illustrate white fragility and how it holds racism in place. These responses spur the daily frustrations and indignities people of color endure from white people who see themselves as open-minded and thus not racist. This book is intended for us, for white progressives who so often—despite our conscious intentions—make life so difficult for people of color. I believe that *white progressives cause the most daily damage to people of color*. I define a white progressive as any white person who thinks he or she is not racist, or is less racist, or in the "choir," or already "gets it." White progressives can be the most difficult for people of color because, to the degree that we think we have arrived, we will put our energy into making sure that others see us as having arrived. None of our energy will go into what we need to be doing for the rest of our lives: engaging in ongoing self-awareness, continuing education, relationship building, and actual antiracist practice. White progressives do indeed uphold and perpetrate racism, but our defensiveness and certitude make it virtually impossible to explain to us how we do so.

Racism has been among the most complex social dilemmas since the founding of this country. While there is no biological race as we understand it (see chapter 2), race as a social construct has profound significance and shapes every aspect of our lives.[1] Race will influence whether we will survive our birth, where we are most likely to live, which schools we will attend, who our friends and partners will be, what careers we will have, how much money we will earn, how healthy we will be, and even how long we can expect to live.[2] This book does not attempt to provide the solution to racism. Nor does it attempt to prove that racism exists; I start from that premise. My goal is to make visible how one aspect of white sensibility continues to hold racism in place: white fragility.

I will explain the phenomenon of white fragility, how we develop it, how it protects racial inequality, and what we might do about it.

CHAPTER 1

THE CHALLENGES OF TALKING TO WHITE PEOPLE ABOUT RACISM

WE DON'T SEE OURSELVES IN RACIAL TERMS

I am a white American raised in the United States. I have a white frame of reference and a white worldview, and I move through the world with a white experience. My experience is not a universal human experience. It is a particularly white experience in a society in which race matters profoundly; a society that is deeply separate and unequal by race. However, like most white people raised in the US, I was not taught to see myself in racial terms and certainly not to draw attention to my race or to behave as if it mattered in any way. Of course, I was made aware that *somebody's* race mattered, and if race was discussed, it would be theirs, not mine. Yet a critical component of cross-racial skill building is the ability to sit with the discomfort of being seen racially, of having to proceed as if our race matters (which it does). Being seen racially is a common trigger of white fragility, and thus, to build our stamina, white people must face the first challenge: naming our race.

OUR OPINIONS ARE UNINFORMED

I have never met a white person without an opinion on racism. It's not really possible to grow up in the United States or spend any significant time here—or any other culture with a history of Western colonization—without developing opinions on racism. And white people's opinions on racism tend to be strong. Yet race relations are profoundly complex. We must be willing to consider that unless we have devoted intentional and ongoing study, our opinions are necessarily uninformed, even ignorant. How can I say that if you are white, your opinions on racism are most likely ignorant, when I don't even know you? I can say so because nothing in mainstream US culture gives us the information we need to have the nuanced understanding of arguably the most complex and enduring social dynamic of the last several hundred years.

For example, I can be seen as qualified to lead a major or minor organization in this country with no understanding whatsoever of the perspectives or experiences of people of color, few if any relationships with people of color, and virtually no ability to engage critically with the topic of race. I can get through graduate school without ever discussing racism. I can graduate from law school without ever discussing racism. I can get through a teacher-education program without ever discussing racism. If I am in a program considered progressive, I might have a single required "diversity" course. A handful of faculty will have fought for years to get me this course, likely having had to overcome resistance from the majority of their white colleagues, and will still be fighting to keep the course. In this diversity course, we might read "ethnic" authors and learn about heroes and heroines from various groups of color, but there's no guarantee we'll discuss racism.

In fact, when we try to talk openly and honestly about race, white fragility quickly emerges as we are so often met with silence, defensiveness, argumentation, certitude, and other forms of pushback. These are not natural responses; they are social forces that prevent us from attaining the racial knowledge we need to engage more productively, and they function powerfully to hold the racial hierarchy in place. These forces include the ideologies of individualism and meritocracy, narrow and repetitive media representations of people of color, segregation in schools and neighborhoods, depictions of whiteness as the human ideal, truncated history, jokes and warnings, taboos on openly talking about race, and white solidarity.

Interrupting the forces of racism is ongoing, lifelong work because the forces conditioning us into racist frameworks are always at play; our learning will never be finished. Yet our simplistic definition of racism—as intentional acts of racial discrimination committed by immoral individuals—engenders a confidence that we are not part of the problem and that our learning is thus complete. The claims we offer up as evidence are implausible. For example, perhaps you've heard someone say "I was taught to treat everyone the same" or "People just need to be taught to respect one another, and that begins in the home." These statements tend to end the discussion and the learning that could come from sustained engagement. Further, they are unconvincing to most people of color and only invalidate their experiences. Many white people simply do not understand the process of socialization, and this is our next challenge.

WE DON'T UNDERSTAND SOCIALIZATION

When I talk to white people about racism, their responses are so predictable I sometimes feel as though we are all reciting lines from a shared script. And on some level, we are, because we are actors in a shared culture. A significant aspect of the white script derives from our seeing ourselves as both objective and unique. To understand white fragility, we have to begin to understand why we cannot fully be either; we must understand the forces of socialization.

We make sense of perceptions and experiences through our particular cultural lens. This lens is neither universal nor objective, and without it, a person could not function in any human society. But exploring these cultural frameworks can be particularly challenging in Western culture precisely because of two key Western ideologies: individualism and objectivity. Briefly, individualism holds that we are each unique and stand apart from others, even those within our social groups. Objectivity tells us that it is possible to be free of all bias. These ideologies make it very difficult for white people to explore the collective aspects of the white experience.

Individualism is a story line that creates, communicates, reproduces, and reinforces the concept that each of us is a unique individual and that our group memberships, such as race, class, or gender, are irrelevant to our opportunities. Individualism claims that there are no intrinsic barriers to individual success and that failure is not a consequence of social structures but comes from individual character. According to the ideology of individualism, race is irrelevant. Of course, we do occupy distinct race, gender, class, and other positions that profoundly shape our life chances in ways that are not natural, voluntary, or random; opportunity is not equally distributed across race, class, and gender. On some level, we know that Bill Gates's son was born into a set of opportunities that will benefit him throughout his life, whether he is mediocre or exceptional. Yet even though Gates's son has clearly been handed unearned advantage, we cling tightly to the ideology of individualism when asked to consider our own unearned advantages.

Regardless of our protestations that social groups don't matter and that we see everyone as equal, we know that to be a man as defined by the dominant culture is a different experience from being a woman. We know that to be viewed as old is different from being viewed as young, rich is different from poor, able-bodied different from having a disability, gay different from heterosexual, and so on. These groups matter, but they don't matter naturally, as we are often taught to believe. Rather, we are taught that they matter, and the social meaning ascribed to these groups creates a difference in lived experience. We are taught these social meanings in myriad ways, by a range of people, and through a variety of mediums. This training continues after childhood and throughout our lives. Much of it is nonverbal and is achieved through watching and comparing ourselves to others.

We are socialized into these groups collectively. In mainstream culture, we all receive the same messages about what these groups mean, why being in one group is a different experience from being in another. And we also know that it is "better" to be in one of these groups than to be in its opposite—for example, to be young rather than old, able-bodied rather than have a disability, rich rather than poor. We gain our understanding of group meaning collectively through aspects of the society around us that are shared and unavoidable: television, movies, news items, song lyrics, magazines, textbooks, schools, religion, literature, stories, jokes, traditions and practices, history, and so on. These dimensions of our culture shape our group identities.

Our understanding of ourselves is necessarily based on our comparisons with others. The concept of pretty has no meaning without the concept of ugly, smart means little without the idea of not-smart or "stupid," and deserving has no meaning without the concept of undeserving. We come to understand who we are by understanding who we are not. But because of our society's emphasis on individuality, many of us are unskilled at reflecting on our group memberships. To understand race relations today, we must push against our conditioning and grapple with how and why racial group memberships matter.

In addition to challenging our sense of ourselves as individuals, tackling group identity also challenges our belief in objectivity. If group membership is relevant, then we don't see the world from the universal human perspective but from the perspective of a particular kind of human. In this way, both ideologies are disrupted. Thus, reflecting on our racial frames is particularly challenging for many white people, because we are taught that to have a racial viewpoint is to be biased. Unfortunately, this belief protects our biases, because denying that we have them ensures that we won't examine or change them. This will be important to remember when we consider our racial socialization, because there is a vast difference between what we verbally tell our children and all the other ways we train them into the racial norms of our culture.

For many white people, the mere title of this book will cause resistance because I am breaking a cardinal rule of individualism—*I am generalizing*. I am proceeding as if I could know anything about someone just because the person is white. Right now you may be thinking of all the ways that you are different from other white people and that if I just knew how you had come to this country, or were close to these people, grew up in this neighborhood, endured this struggle, or had this experience, then I would know that you were different—that you were not racist. I've witnessed this common reflex countless times in my work.

For example, I recently gave a talk to a group of about two hundred employees. There were no more than five people of color in their organization, and of these five, only two were African American. Over and over, I emphasized the importance of white people having racial humility and of not exempting ourselves from the unavoidable dynamics of racism. As soon as I was done speaking, a line of white people formed—ostensibly to ask me questions—but more typically to reiterate the same opinions on race they held when they had entered the room. The first in line was a white man who explained that he was Italian American and that Italians were once considered black and discriminated against, so didn't I think that white people experience racism too? That he could be in that overwhelmingly white room of coworkers and exempt himself from an examination of his whiteness because Italians were once discriminated against is an all-too-common example of individualism. A more fruitful form of engagement (because it expands rather than protects his current worldview) would have been to consider how Italian Americans were able to become white and how that assimilation has shaped his experiences in the present *as a white man*. His claims did not illustrate that he was different from other white people when it comes to race. I can predict that many readers will make similar claims of exception precisely because we are products of our culture, not separate from it.

As a sociologist, I am quite comfortable generalizing; social life is patterned and predictable in measurable ways. But I understand that my generalizations may cause some defensiveness for the white people about whom I am generalizing, given how cherished the ideology of individualism is in our culture. There are, of course, exceptions, but patterns are recognized as such precisely because they are recurring and predictable. We cannot understand modern forms of racism if we cannot or will not explore patterns of group behavior and their effects on individuals. I ask readers to make the specific adjustments they think are necessary to their situation, rather than reject the evidence entirely. For example, perhaps you grew up in poverty, or are an Ashkenazi Jew of European heritage, or were raised in a military family. Perhaps you grew up in Canada, Hawaii, or Germany, or had people of color in your family. None of these situations exempts you from the forces of racism, because no aspect of society is outside of these forces.

Rather than use what you see as unique about yourself as an exemption from further examination, a more fruitful approach would be to ask yourself, "I am white and I have had X experience. How did X shape me as a result of *also being white*?" Setting aside your sense of uniqueness is a critical skill that will allow you to see the big picture of the society in which we live; individualism will not. For now, try to let go of your individual narrative and grapple with the collective messages we all receive as members of a larger shared culture. Work to see how these messages have shaped your life, rather than use some aspect of your story to excuse yourself from their impact.

WE HAVE A SIMPLISTIC UNDERSTANDING OF RACISM

The final challenge we need to address is our definition of "racist." In the post–civil rights era, we have been taught that racists are mean people who intentionally dislike others because of their race; racists are immoral. Therefore, if I am saying that my readers are racist or, even worse, that all white people are racist, I am saying something deeply offensive; I am questioning my readers' very moral character. How can I make this claim when I don't even know my readers? Many of you have friends and loved ones of color, so how can you be racist? In fact, since it's racist to generalize about people according to race, I am the one being racist! So let me be clear: If your definition of a racist is someone who holds conscious dislike of people because of race, then I agree that it is offensive for me to suggest that you are racist when I don't know you. I also agree that if this is your definition of racism, and you are against racism, then you are not racist. Now breathe. I am not using this definition of racism, and I am not saying that you are immoral. If you can remain open as I lay out my argument, it should soon begin to make sense.

In light of the challenges raised here, I expect that white readers will have moments of discomfort reading this book. This feeling may be a sign that I've managed to unsettle the racial status quo, which is my goal. The racial status quo is comfortable for white people, and we will not move forward in race relations if we remain comfortable. The key to moving forward is what we do with our discomfort. We can use it as a door out—blame the messenger and disregard the message. Or we can use it as a door in by asking, Why does this unsettle me? What would it mean for me if this were true? How does this lens change my understanding of racial dynamics? How can my unease help reveal the unexamined assumptions I have been making? Is it possible that because I am white, there are some racial dynamics that I can't see? Am I willing to consider that possibility? If I am not willing to do so, then why not?

If you are reading this and are still making your case for why you are different from other white people and why none of this applies to you, stop and take a breath. Now return to the questions above, and keep working through them. To interrupt white fragility, we need to build our capacity to sustain the discomfort of not knowing, the discomfort of being racially unmoored, the discomfort of racial humility. Our next task is to understand how the forces of racial socialization are constantly at play. The inability to acknowledge these forces inevitably leads to the resistance and defensiveness of white fragility. To increase the racial stamina that counters white fragility, we must reflect on the whole of our identities—and our racial group identity in particular. For white people, this means first struggling with what it means to be white.

CHAPTER 2

RACISM AND WHITE SUPREMACY

Many of us have been taught to believe that there are distinct biological and genetic differences between races. This biology accounts for visual differences such as skin color, hair texture, and eye shape, and traits that we believe we see such as sexuality, athleticism, or mathematical ability. The idea of race as a biological construct makes it easy to believe that many of the divisions we see in society are natural. But race, like gender, is socially constructed. The differences we see with our eyes—differences such as hair texture and eye color—are superficial and emerged as adaptations to geography.[1] Under the skin, there is no true biological race. The external characteristics that we use to define race are unreliable indicators of genetic variation between any two people.[2]

However, the belief that race and the differences associated with it are biological is deep-seated. To challenge the belief in race as biology, we need to understand the social and economic investments that drove science to organize society and its resources along racial lines and why this organization is so enduring.

SOCIAL CONSTRUCTION OF RACE IN THE UNITED STATES

Freedom and equality—regardless of religion or class status—were radical new ideas when the United States was formed. At the same time, the US economy was based on the abduction and enslavement of African people, the displacement and genocide of Indigenous people, and the annexation of Mexican lands. Further, the colonizers who came were not free of their own cultural conditioning; they brought with them deeply internalized patterns of domination and submission.[3]

The tension between the noble ideology of equality and the cruel reality of genocide, enslavement, and colonization had to be reconciled. Thomas Jefferson (who himself owned hundreds of enslaved people) and others turned to science. Jefferson suggested that there were natural differences between the races and asked scientists to find them.[4] If science could prove that black people were naturally and inherently inferior (he saw Indigenous people as culturally deficient—a shortcoming that could be remedied), there would be no contradiction between our professed ideals and our actual practices. There were, of course, enormous economic interests in justifying enslavement and colonization. Race science was driven by these social and economic interests, which came to establish cultural norms and legal rulings that legitimized racism and the privileged status of those defined as white.

Drawing on the work of Europeans before them, American scientists began searching for the answer to the perceived inferiority of non-Anglo groups. Illustrating the power of our questions to shape the knowledge we validate, these scientists didn't ask, "Are blacks (and others) inferior?" They asked, "Why are blacks (and others) inferior?" In less than a century, Jefferson's suggestion of racial difference became commonly accepted scientific "fact."[5]

The idea of racial inferiority was created to justify unequal treatment; belief in racial inferiority is not what triggered unequal treatment. Nor was fear of difference. As Ta-Nehisi Coates states, "But race is the child of racism, not the father."[6] He means that first we exploited people for their resources, not according to how they looked. Exploitation came first, and then the ideology of unequal races to justify this exploitation followed. Similarly, historian Ibram Kendi, in his National Book Award–winning work *Stamped from the Beginning*, explains: "The beneficiaries of slavery, segregation, and mass incarceration have produced racist ideas of Black people being best suited for or deserving of the confines of slavery, segregation, or the jail cell. Consumers of these racist ideas have been led to believe there is something wrong with Black people, and not the policies that have enslaved, oppressed, and confined so many Black people."[7] Kendi goes on to argue that if we truly believe that all humans are equal, then disparity in condition can only be the result of systemic discrimination.

THE PERCEPTION OF RACE

Race is an evolving social idea that was created to legitimize racial inequality and protect white advantage. The term "white" first appeared in colonial law in the late 1600s. By 1790, people were asked to claim their race on the census, and by 1825, the perceived degrees of blood determined who would be classified as Indian. From the late 1800s through the early twentieth century, as waves of immigrants entered the United States, the concept of a white race was solidified.[8]

When slavery in the United States was abolished in 1865, whiteness remained profoundly important as legalized racist exclusion and violence against African Americans continued in new forms. To have citizenship—and the rights citizenship imbued—you had to be legally classified as white. People with nonwhite racial classifications began to petition the courts to be reclassified. Now the courts were in the position to decide who was white and who was not. For example, Armenians won their case to be reclassified as white with the help of a scientific witness who claimed they were scientifically "Caucasian." In 1922, the Supreme Court ruled that the Japanese could not be legally white, because they were scientifically classified as "Mongoloid." A year later, the court stated that Asian Indians were not legally white, even though they were also scientifically classified as "Caucasian." To justify these contradictory rulings, the court stated that being white was based on the common understanding of the white man. In other words, people already seen as white got to decide who was white.[9]

The metaphor of the United States as the great melting pot, in which immigrants from around the world come together and melt into one unified society through the process of assimilation, is a cherished idea. Once new immigrants learn English and adapt to American culture and customs, they become Americans. In reality, only European immigrants were allowed to melt, or assimilate, into dominant culture in the nineteenth and twentieth centuries, because, regardless of their ethnic identities, these immigrants were perceived to be white and thus could belong.

Race is a social construction, and thus who is included in the category of white changes over time. As the Italian American man from my workshop noted, European ethnic groups such as the Irish, Italian, and Polish were excluded in the past. But where they may have been originally divided in terms of origin, European immigrants became racially united through assimilation.[10] This process of assimilation—speaking English, eating "American" foods, discarding customs that set them apart—reified the perception of American as white. Racial identification in the larger society plays a fundamental role in identity development, in how we see ourselves.

If we "look white," we are treated as white in society at large. For example, people of southern European heritage, such as Spanish or Portuguese, or from the former Soviet Union, especially if they are new immigrants or were raised by immigrants, are likely to have a stronger sense of ethnic identity than will someone of the same ethnicity whose ancestors have been here for generations. Yet although their internal identity may be different, if they "pass" as white, they will still have a white experience externally. If they look white, the default assumption will be that they are white and thus they will be responded to as white. The incongruity between their internal ethnic identity (e.g., Portuguese, Spanish) and external racial experience (white) would provide a more complex or nuanced sense of identity than that of someone who doesn't have a strong ethnic identity. However, they are still granted white status and the advantages that come with that status. Today, these advantages are de facto rather than de jure, but are nonetheless powerful in shaping our daily lives. It is on each of us who pass as white to identify how these advantages shape us, not to deny them wholescale.

Because race is a product of social forces, it has also manifested itself along class lines; poor and working-class people were not always perceived as fully white.[11] In a society that grants fewer opportunities to those not seen as white, economic and racial forces are inseparable. However, poor and working-class whites were eventually granted full entry into whiteness as a way to exploit labor. If poor whites were focused on feeling superior to those below them in status, they were less focused on those above. The poor and working classes, if united across race, could be a powerful force. But racial divisions have served to keep them from organizing against the owning class who profits from their labor.[12] Still, although working-class whites experience classism, they aren't also experiencing racism. I grew up in poverty and felt a deep sense of shame about being poor. But I also always knew that I was white, and that it was better to be white.

RACISM

To understand racism, we need to first distinguish it from mere prejudice and discrimination. Prejudice is pre-judgment about another person based on the social groups to which that person belongs. Prejudice consists of thoughts and feelings, including stereotypes, attitudes, and generalizations that are based on little or no experience and then are projected onto everyone from that group. Our prejudices tend to be shared because we swim in the same cultural water and absorb the same messages.

All humans have prejudice; we cannot avoid it. If I am aware that a social group exists, I will have gained information about that group from the society around me. This information helps me make sense of the group from my cultural framework. People who claim not to be prejudiced are demonstrating a profound lack of self-awareness. Ironically, they are also demonstrating the power of socialization—we have all been taught in schools, through movies, and from family members, teachers, and clergy that it is important not to be prejudiced. Unfortunately, the prevailing belief that prejudice is bad causes us to deny its unavoidable reality.

Prejudice is foundational to understanding white fragility because suggesting that white people have racial prejudice is perceived as saying that we are bad and should be ashamed. We then feel the need to defend our character rather than explore the inevitable racial prejudices we have absorbed so that we might change them. In this way, our misunderstanding about what prejudice is protects it.

Discrimination is *action* based on prejudice. These actions include ignoring, exclusion, threats, ridicule, slander, and violence. For example, if hatred is the emotion we feel because of our prejudice, extreme acts of discrimination, such as violence, may follow. These forms of discrimination are generally clear and recognizable. But if what we feel is more subtle, such as mild discomfort, the discrimination is likely to also be subtle, even hard to detect. Most of us can acknowledge that we do feel some unease around certain groups of people, if only a heightened sense of self-consciousness. But this feeling doesn't come naturally. Our unease comes from living separate from a group of people while simultaneously absorbing incomplete or erroneous information about them. When the prejudice causes me to act differently—I am less relaxed around you or I avoid interacting with you—I am now discriminating. Prejudice always manifests itself in action because the way I see the world drives my actions in the world. Everyone has prejudice, and everyone discriminates. Given this reality, inserting the qualifier "reverse" is nonsensical.

When a racial group's collective prejudice is backed by the power of legal authority and institutional control, it is transformed into racism, a far-reaching system that functions independently from the intentions or self-images of individual actors. J. Kēhaulani Kauanui, professor of American studies and anthropology at Wesleyan University, explains, "Racism is a structure, not an event."[13] American women's struggle for suffrage illustrates how institutional power transforms prejudice and discrimination into structures of oppression. Everyone has prejudice and discriminates, but structures of oppression go well beyond individuals. While women could be prejudiced and discriminate against men in individual interactions, women as a group could not deny men their civil rights. But men as a group could and did deny women their civil rights. Men could do so because they controlled all the institutions. Therefore, the only way women could gain suffrage was for men to grant it to them; women could not grant suffrage to themselves.

Similarly, racism—like sexism and other forms of oppression—occurs when a racial group's prejudice is backed by legal authority and institutional control. This authority and control transforms individual prejudices into a far-reaching system that no longer depends on the good intentions of individual actors; it becomes the default of the society and is reproduced automatically. Racism is a system. And I would be remiss if I did not acknowledge the intersection of race and gender in the example of suffrage; *white* men granted suffrage to women, but only granted full access to white women. Women of color were denied full access until the Voting Rights Act of 1964.

The system of racism begins with ideology, which refers to the big ideas that are reinforced throughout society. From birth, we are conditioned into accepting and not questioning these ideas. Ideology is reinforced across society, for example, in schools and textbooks, political speeches, movies, advertising, holiday celebrations, and words and phrases. These ideas are also reinforced through social penalties when someone questions an ideology and through the limited availability of alternative ideas. Ideologies are the frameworks through which we are taught to represent, interpret, understand, and make sense of social existence.[14] Because these ideas are constantly reinforced, they are very hard to avoid believing and internalizing. Examples of ideology in the United States include individualism, the superiority of capitalism as an economic system and democracy as a political system, consumerism as a desirable lifestyle, and meritocracy (anyone can succeed if he or she works hard).

The racial ideology that circulates in the United States rationalizes racial hierarchies as the outcome of a natural order resulting from either genetics or individual effort or talent. Those who don't succeed are just not as naturally capable, deserving, or hardworking. Ideologies that obscure racism as a system of inequality are perhaps the most powerful racial forces because once we accept our positions within racial hierar-chies, these positions seem natural and difficult to question, even when we are disadvantaged by them. In this way, very little external pres-sure needs to be applied to keep people in their places; once the ratio-nalizations for inequality are internalized, both sides will uphold the relationship.

Racism is deeply embedded in the fabric of our society. It is not limited to a single act or person. Nor does it move back and forth, one day benefiting whites and another day (or even era) benefiting people of color. The direction of power between white people and people of color is historic, traditional, and normalized in ideology. Racism differs from individual racial prejudice and racial discrimination in the historical accumulation and ongoing use of institutional power and authority to support the prejudice and to systematically enforce discriminatory be-haviors with far-reaching effects.

People of color may also hold prejudices and discriminate against white people, but they lack the social and institutional power that trans-forms their prejudice and discrimination into racism; the impact of their prejudice on whites is temporary and contextual. Whites hold the social and institutional positions in society to infuse their racial prejudice into the laws, policies, practices, and norms of society in a way that people of color do not. A person of color may refuse to wait on me if I enter a shop, but people of color cannot pass legislation that prohibits me and everyone like me from buying a home in a certain neighborhood.

People of color may also hold prejudices and discriminate against their own and other groups of color, but this bias ultimately holds them down and, in this way, reinforces the system of racism that still benefits whites. Racism is a society-wide dynamic that occurs at the group level. When I say that only whites can be racist, I mean that in the United States, only whites have the collective social and institutional power and privilege over people of color. People of color do not have this power and privilege over white people.

Many whites see racism as a thing of the past, and of course, we are well served not to acknowledge it in the present. Yet racial disparity between whites and people of color continues to exist in every institution across society, and in many cases is increasing rather than decreasing. Although segregation may make these disparities difficult for whites to see and easy to deny, racial disparities and their effects on overall quality of life have been extensively documented by a wide range of agencies. Among those documenting these challenges are the US Census Bureau, the United Nations, academic groups such as the UCLA Civil Rights Project and the Metropolis Project, and nonprofits such as the NAACP and the Anti-Defamation League.[15]

Scholar Marilyn Frye uses the metaphor of a birdcage to describe the interlocking forces of oppression.[16] If you stand close to a birdcage and press your face against the wires, your perception of the bars will disappear and you will have an almost unobstructed view of the bird. If you turn your head to examine one wire of the cage closely, you will not be able to see the other wires. If your understanding of the cage is based on this myopic view, you may not understand why the bird doesn't just go around the single wire and fly away. You might even assume that the bird liked or chose its place in the cage.

But if you stepped back and took a wider view, you would begin to see that the wires come together in an interlocking pattern—a pattern that works to hold the bird firmly in place. It now becomes clear that a network of systematically related barriers surrounds the bird. Taken individually, none of these barriers would be that difficult for the bird to get around, but because they interlock with each other, they thoroughly restrict the bird. While some birds may escape from the cage, most will not. And certainly those that do escape will have to navigate many barriers that birds outside the cage do not.

The birdcage metaphor helps us understand why racism can be so hard to see and recognize: we have a limited view. Without recognizing how our position in relation to the bird defines how much of the cage we can see, we rely on single situations, exceptions, and anecdotal evidence for our understanding, rather than on broader, interlocking patterns. Although there are always exceptions, the patterns are consistent and well documented: People of color are confined and shaped by forces and barriers that are not accidental, occasional, or avoidable. These forces are systematically related to each other in ways that restrict their movement.

Individual whites may be "against" racism, but they still benefit from a system that privileges whites as a group. David Wellman succinctly summarizes racism as "a system of advantage based on race."[17] These advantages are referred to as *white privilege*, a sociological concept referring to advantages that are taken for granted by whites and that cannot be similarly enjoyed by people of color in the same context (government, community, workplace, schools, etc.).[18] But let me be clear: stating that racism privileges whites does not mean that individual white people do not struggle or face barriers. It does mean that we do not face the particular barriers of racism.

As with prejudice and discrimination, we can remove the qualifier *reverse* from any discussion of racism. By definition, racism is a deeply embedded historical system of institutional power. It is not fluid and does not change direction simply because a few individuals of color manage to excel.

WHITENESS AS A POSITION OF STATUS

Being perceived as white carries more than a mere racial classification; it is a social and institutional status and identity imbued with legal, political, economic, and social rights and privileges that are denied to others. Reflecting on the social and economic advantages of being classified as white, critical race scholar Cheryl Harris coined the phrase "whiteness as property." Tracing the evolving concept of whiteness across legal history, she explains:

> By according whiteness an actual legal status, an aspect of identity was converted into an external object of property, moving whiteness from privileged identity to a vested interest. The law's construction of whiteness defined and affirmed critical aspects of identity (who is white); of

privilege (what benefits accrue to that status); and, of property (what legal entitlements arise from that status). Whiteness at various times signifies and is deployed as identity, status, and property, sometimes singularly, sometimes in tandem.[19]

Harris's analysis is useful because it shows how identity and perceptions of identity can grant or deny resources. These resources include self-worth, visibility, positive expectations, psychological freedom from the tether of race, freedom of movement, the sense of belonging, and a sense of entitlement to all the above.

We might think of whiteness as all the aspects of being white—aspects that go beyond mere physical differences and are related to the meaning and resultant material advantage of being defined as white in society: what is granted and how it is granted based on that meaning. Instead of the typical focus on how racism hurts people of color, to examine whiteness is to focus on how racism elevates white people.

Whiteness rests upon a foundational premise: the definition of whites as the norm or standard for human, and people of color as a deviation from that norm. Whiteness is not acknowledged by white people, and the white reference point is assumed to be universal and is imposed on everyone. White people find it very difficult to think about whiteness as a specific state of being that could have an impact on one's life and perceptions.

People of color, including W. E. B. Du Bois and James Baldwin, have been writing about whiteness for decades, if not centuries. These writers urged white people to turn their attention onto themselves to explore what it means to be white in a society that is so divided by race. For example, in 1946, a French reporter asked expatriate writer Richard Wright his thoughts on the "Negro problem" in the United States. Wright replied, "There isn't any Negro problem; there is only a white problem."[20]

As Wright pointed out, racism against people of color doesn't occur in a vacuum. Yet the idea that racism in the United States can operate outside white people is reinforced through celebrations such as Black History Month, in which we study the Civil War and civil rights eras as if they occurred separately from all US history. In addition to the general way these color-based celebrations take whites out of the equation, there are specific ways that the achievements of people of color are separated from the overall social context and depoliticized, for instance, in stories we tell about black cultural heroes.

The story of Jackie Robinson is a classic example of how whiteness obscures racism by rendering whites, white privilege, and racist institutions invisible. Robinson is often celebrated as the first African American to break the color line and play in major-league baseball. While Robinson was certainly an amazing baseball player, this story line depicts him as racially special, a black man who broke the color line himself. The subtext is that Robinson finally had what it took to play with whites, as if no black athlete before him was strong enough to compete at that level. Imagine if instead, the story went something like this: "Jackie Robinson, the first black man whites allowed to play major-league baseball." This version makes a critical distinction because no matter how fantastic a player Robinson was, he simply could not play in the major leagues if whites—who controlled the institution—did not allow it. Were he to walk onto the field before being granted permission by white owners and policy makers, the police would have removed him.

Narratives of racial exceptionality obscure the reality of ongoing institutional white control while reinforcing the ideologies of individualism and meritocracy. They also do whites a disservice by obscuring the white allies who, behind the scenes, worked hard and long to open the field to African American players. These allies could serve as much-needed role models for other whites (although we also need to acknowledge that in the case of the desegregation of baseball, there was an economic incentive for these allies).

I am not against Black History Month. But it should be celebrated in a way that doesn't reinforce whiteness. For those who ask why there is no White History Month, the answer illustrates how whiteness works. White history is implied in the absence of its acknowledgment; white history is the norm for history. Thus, our need to qualify that we are speaking about black history or women's history suggests that these contributions lie outside the norm.

Ruth Frankenberg, a premier white scholar in the field of whiteness studies, describes whiteness as multidimensional. These dimensions include a location of structural advantage, a standpoint from which white people look at ourselves, at others, and at society, and a set of cultural practices that are not named or acknowledged.[21] To say that whiteness is a location of structural advantage is to recognize that to be white is to be in a privileged position within society and its institutions—to be seen as an insider and to be granted the benefits of belonging. This position automatically bestows unearned advantages. Whites control all major institutions of society and set the policies and practices that others must live by. Although rare individual people of color may be inside the circles of power—Colin Powell, Clarence Thomas, Marco Rubio, Barack Obama—they support the status quo and do not challenge racism in any way significant enough to be threatening. Their positions of power do not mean these public figures don't experience racism (Obama endured insults and resistance previously unheard-of), but the status quo remains intact.

To say that whiteness is a standpoint is to say that a significant aspect of white identity is to see oneself as an individual, outside or innocent of race—"just human." This standpoint views white people and their interests as central to, and representative of, humanity. Whites also produce and reinforce the dominant narratives of society—such as individualism and meritocracy—and use these narratives to explain the positions of other racial groups. These narratives allow us to congratulate ourselves on our success within the institutions of society and blame others for their lack of success.

To say that that whiteness includes a set of cultural practices that are not recognized by white people is to understand racism as a network of norms and actions that consistently create advantage for whites and disadvantage for people of color. These norms and actions include basic rights and benefits of the doubt, purportedly granted to all but which are actually only consistently afforded to white people. The dimensions of racism benefiting white people are usually invisible to whites. We are unaware of, or do not acknowledge, the meaning of race and its impact on our own lives. Thus we do not recognize or admit to white privilege and the norms that produce and maintain it. It follows that to name whiteness, much less suggest that it has meaning and grants unearned advantage, will be deeply disconcerting and destabilizing, thus triggering the protective responses of white fragility.

WHITE SUPREMACY

When we look back to the civil rights movement of the 1950s and 1960s, we might think of white supremacists as the people we saw in photos and on television, beating blacks at lunch counters, bombing black churches, and screaming at little Ruby Bridges, the first African American child to integrate an all-white elementary school in Louisiana in 1960. Today we might think of the self-described "alt-right" white nationalists marching with torches in Virginia and shouting "blood and soil" as they protest the removal of Confederate war memorials. Most white people do not identify with these images of white supremacists and so take great umbrage to the term being used more broadly. For sociologists and those involved in current racial justice movements, however, white supremacy is a descriptive and useful term to capture the all-encompassing centrality and assumed superiority of people defined and perceived as white and the practices based on this assumption. White supremacy in this context does not refer to individual white people and their individual intentions or actions but to an overarching political, economic, and social system of domination. Again, racism is a structure, not an event. While hate groups that openly proclaim white superiority do exist and this term refers to them also, the popular consciousness solely associates *white supremacy* with these radical groups. This reductive definition obscures the reality of the larger system at work and prevents us from addressing this system.

While racism in other cultures exists based on different ideas of which racial group is superior to another, the United States is a global power, and through movies and mass media, corporate culture, advertising, US-owned manufacturing, military presence, historical colonial relations, missionary work, and other means, white supremacy is circulated globally. This powerful ideology promotes the idea of whiteness as the ideal for humanity well beyond the West. White supremacy is especially relevant in countries that have a history of colonialism by Western nations.

In his book *The Racial Contract*, Charles W. Mills argues that the racial contract is a tacit and sometimes explicit agreement among members of the peoples of Europe to assert, promote, and maintain the ideal of white supremacy in relation to all other people of the world. This agreement is an intentional and integral characteristic of the social contract, underwriting all other social contracts. White supremacy has shaped a system of global European domination: it brings into existence whites and nonwhites, full persons and subpersons. It influences white moral theory and moral psychology and is imposed on nonwhites through ideological conditioning and violence. Mills says that "what has usually been taken . . . as the racist 'exception' has really been the rule; what has been taken as the 'rule' . . . [racial equality] . . . has really been the exception."[22]

Mills describes white supremacy as "the unnamed political system that has made the modern world what it is today."[23] He notes that although white supremacy has shaped Western political thought for hundreds of years, it is never named. In this way, white supremacy is rendered invisible while other political systems—socialism, capitalism, fascism—are identified and studied. In fact, much of white supremacy's power is drawn from its invisibility, the taken-for-granted aspects that underwrite all other political and social contracts.

Mills makes two points that are critical to our understanding of white fragility. First, white supremacy is never acknowledged. Second, we cannot study any sociopolitical system without addressing how that system is mediated by race. The failure to acknowledge white supremacy protects it from examination and holds it in place.

In Ta-Nehisi Coates's essay "The Case for Reparations," he makes a similar point:

> To ignore the fact that one of the oldest republics in the world was erected on a foundation of white supremacy, to pretend that the problems of a dual society are the same as the problems of unregulated capitalism, is to cover the sin of national plunder with the sin of national lying. The lie ignores the fact that reducing American poverty and ending white supremacy are not the same. . . . [W]hite supremacy is not merely the work of hotheaded demagogues, or a matter of false consciousness, but a force so fundamental to America that it is difficult to imagine the country without it.[24]

In light of the reality of historical and continual white supremacy, white complaints about "reverse" racism by programs intended to ameliorate the most basic levels of discrimination are profoundly petty and delusional. As Mills summarizes:

> Both globally and within particular nation states, then, white people, Europeans and their descendants, continue to benefit from the Racial Contract, which creates a world in their cultural image, political states differentially favoring their interests, an economy structured around the racial exploitation of others, and a moral psychology . . . skewed consciously or unconsciously toward privileging them, taking the status quo of differing racial entitlement as normatively legitimate, and not to be investigated further.[25]

Race scholars use the term *white supremacy* to describe a sociopolitical economic system of domination based on racial categories that benefits those defined and perceived as white. This system of structural power privileges, centralizes, and elevates white people as a group. If, for example, we look at the racial breakdown of the people who control our institutions, we see telling numbers in 2016–2017:

- Ten richest Americans: 100 percent white (seven of whom are among the ten richest in the world)
- US Congress: 90 percent white
- US governors: 96 percent white
- Top military advisers: 100 percent white
- President and vice president: 100 percent white
- US House Freedom Caucus: 99 percent white
- Current US presidential cabinet: 91 percent white
- People who decide which TV shows we see: 93 percent white
- People who decide which books we read: 90 percent white
- People who decide which news is covered: 85 percent white
- People who decide which music is produced: 95 percent white
- People who directed the one hundred top-grossing films of all time, worldwide: 95 percent white
- Teachers: 82 percent white
- Full-time college professors: 84 percent white
- Owners of men's professional football teams: 97 percent white[26]

These numbers are not describing minor organizations. Nor are these institutions special-interest groups. The groups listed above are the most powerful in the country. These numbers are not a matter of "good people" versus "bad people." They represent power and control by a racial group that is in the position to disseminate and protect its own self-image, worldview, and interests across the entire society.

One of the most potent ways white supremacy is disseminated is through media representations, which have a profound impact on how we see the world. Those who write and direct films are our cultural narrators; the stories they tell shape our worldviews. Given that the majority of white people live in racial isolation from people of color (and black people in particular) and have very few authentic cross-racial relationships, white people are deeply influenced by the racial messages in films. Consider one statistic from the preceding list: of the hundred top-grossing films worldwide in 2016, ninety-five were directed by white Americans (ninety-nine of them by men). That is an incredibly homogenous group of directors. Because these men are most likely at the top of the social hierarchy in terms of race, class, and gender, they are the least likely to have a wide variety of authentic egalitarian cross-racial relationships. Yet they are in the position to represent the racial "other." Their representations of the "other" are thereby extremely narrow and problematic, and yet they are reinforced over and over. Further, these biased representations have been disseminated worldwide; while white supremacy originated in the West, it circulates globally.

White resistance to the term *white supremacy* prevents us from examining how these messages shape us. Explicit white supremacists understand this. Christian Picciolini, a former white nationalist, explains that white nationalists recognized that they had to distance themselves from the terms *racist* and *white supremacy* to gain broader appeal. He describes the "alt-right" and white nationalist movements as the culmination of a thirty-year effort to massage the white supremacist message: "We recognized back then that we were turning away the average American white racists and that we needed to look and speak more like our neighbors. The idea we had was to blend in, normalize, make the message more palatable."[27] Derek Black, godson of David Duke and former key youth leader in the white nationalist movement, explains: "My whole talk was the fact that you could run as Republicans, and say things like we need to shut down immigration, we need to fight affirmative action, we need to end globalism, and you could win these positions, maybe as long as you didn't get outed as a white nationalist and get all the controversy that comes along with it."[28]

Today's white nationalists are not the first to recognize the importance of distancing oneself from more-explicit expressions of white supremacy. In a 1981 interview, Lee Atwater, Republican political strategist and adviser to presidents Ronald Reagan and George H. W. Bush, explained what came to be known as "the Southern strategy"—how to appeal to the racism of white Southern voters without pronouncing it openly:

> You start out in 1954 by saying, "Nigger, nigger, nigger." By 1968 you can't say "nigger"—that hurts you. Backfires. So you say stuff like forced busing, states' rights and all that stuff. You're getting so abstract now [that] you're talking about cutting taxes, and all these things you're talking about are totally economic things and a byproduct of them is [that] blacks get hurt worse than whites. And subconsciously maybe that is part of it. . . . But I'm saying that if it is getting that abstract, and that coded, that we are doing away with the racial problem one way or the other. You follow me—because obviously sitting around saying, "We want to cut this," is much more abstract than even the busing thing, and a hell of a lot more abstract than "Nigger, nigger."[29]

Our umbrage at the term *white supremacy* only serves to protect the processes it describes and obscure the mechanisms of racial inequality. Still, I understand that the term is very charged for many white people, especially older white people who associate the term with extreme hate groups. However, I hope to have made clear that white supremacy is something much more pervasive and subtle than the actions of explicit white nationalists. White supremacy describes the culture we live in, a culture that positions white people and all that is associated with them (whiteness) as ideal. White supremacy is more than the idea that whites are superior to people of color; it is the deeper premise that supports this idea—the definition of whites as the norm or standard for human, and people of color as a deviation from that norm.

Naming white supremacy changes the conversation in two key ways: It makes the system visible and shifts the locus of change onto white people, where it belongs. It also points us in the direction of the lifelong work that is uniquely ours, challenging our complicity with and investment in racism. This does not mean that people of color do not play a part but that the full weight of responsibility rests with those who control the institutions.

THE WHITE RACIAL FRAME

Sociologist Joe Feagin coined the term "white racial frame" to describe how whites circulate and reinforce racial messages that position whites as superior.[30] In this way, the white racial frame rests on, and is a key mechanism of, white supremacy. The frame is deep and extensive, with thousands of stored "bits." These bits are pieces of cultural information—images, stories, interpretations, omissions, silences—that are passed along from one person and group to the next, and from one generation to the next. The bits circulate both explicitly and implicitly, for example, through movies, television, news, and other media and stories told to us by family and friends. By constantly using the white racial frame to interpret social relations and integrating new bits, whites reinscribe the frame ever deeper.

At the most general level, the racial frame views whites as superior in culture and achievement and views people of color as generally of less social, economic, and political consequence; people of color are seen as inferior to whites in the making and keeping of the nation. At the next level of framing, because social institutions (education, medicine, law, government, finance, and the military) are controlled by whites, white dominance is unremarkable and taken for granted. That whites are disproportionately enriched and privileged via these institutions is also taken for granted; we are entitled to more privileges and resources because we are "better" people. At the deepest level of the white frame, negative stereotypes and images of racial others as inferior are reinforced and accepted. At this level, corresponding emotions such as fear, contempt, and resentment are also stored.

The frame includes both negative understandings of people of color and positive understandings of whites and white institutions. It is so internalized, so submerged, that it is never consciously considered or challenged by most whites. To get a sense of the white racial frame below the surface of your conscious awareness, think back to the earliest time that you were aware that people from racial groups other than your own existed. People of color recall a sense of always having been aware, while most white people recall being aware by at least age five. If you lived in a primarily white environment and are having trouble remembering, think about Disney movies, music videos, sports heroes, Chinese food, Aunt Jemima syrup, Uncle Ben's rice, the Taco Bell Chihuahua, Columbus Day, Apu from *The Simpsons*, and the donkey from *Shrek*.

Reflect on these representations and ask yourself, Did your parents tell you that race didn't matter and that everyone was equal? Did they have many friends of color? If people of color did not live in your neighborhood, why didn't they? Where did they live? What images, sounds, and smells did you associate with these other neighborhoods? What kind of activities did you think went on there? Were you encouraged to visit these neighborhoods, or were you discouraged from visiting these neighborhoods?

What about schools? What made a school good? Who went to good schools? Who went to bad schools? If the schools in your area were racially segregated (as most schools in the United States are), why didn't you attend school together? If this is because you lived in different neighborhoods, why did you live in different neighborhoods? Were "their" schools considered equal to, better than, or worse than, yours? If there was busing in your town, in which direction did it go; who was bused into whose schools? Why did the busing go in one direction and not the other?

If you went to school together, did you all sit together in the cafeteria? If not, why not? Were the honors or advanced placement classes and the lower-track classes equally racially integrated? If not, why not?

Now think about your teachers. When was the first time you had a teacher of the same race as yours? Did you often have teachers of the same race as your own?

Most white people, in reflecting on these questions, realize that they almost always had white teachers; many did not have a teacher of color until college. Conversely, most people of color have rarely if ever had a teacher who reflected their own race(s). Why is it important to reflect on our teachers in our effort to uncover our racial socialization and the messages we receive from schools?

As you answer these questions, also consider which races were geographically closer to you than others. If your school was perceived as racially diverse, which races were more represented, and how did the racial distribution affect the sense of value associated with the school? For example, if white and Asian-heritage students were the primary racial groups in your school, your school was likely to be seen as better than a school with more representation from black and Latinx students. What were you learning about the racial hierarchy and your place in it from geography?

If you lived and went to school in racial segregation as most people in the United States do, you had to make sense of the incongruity between the claim that everyone was equal and the lived reality of segregation. If you lived in an integrated neighborhood and/or attended an integrated school, you had to make sense of the segregation in most of society outside the school, especially in segments considered of higher value or quality. It is also highly likely that there was still racial separation within the school. And for those of us who may have grown up in more integrated environments due to social class or changing neighborhood demographics, it is unlikely that integration has been sustained in our current lives. Reflection on these questions provides an entry point into the deeper messages that we all absorb and that shape our behavior and responses below the conscious level.

In the US, race is encoded in geography. I can name every neighborhood in my city and its racial makeup. I can also tell you if a neighborhood is coming up or down in terms of home equity, and this will be based primarily on how its racial demographics are changing. Going up? It will be getting whiter. Going down? It will be getting less white. When I was a child, posters on my school walls and television shows like *Sesame Street* told me explicitly that all people were equal, but we simply do not live together across race. I had to make sense of this separation. If we were equal, why did we live separately? It must be normal and natural to live apart (certainly no adult in my life was complaining about the separation). And at a deeper level, it must be righteous that we live apart, since we are better people. How did I get the message that we were better people? Consider how we talk about white neighborhoods: good, safe, sheltered, clean, desirable. By definition, other spaces (not white) are bad, dangerous, crime-ridden and to be avoided; these neighborhoods are not positioned as sheltered and innocent. In these ways, the white racial frame is under construction.

Predominately white neighborhoods are not outside of race—they are *teeming* with race. Every moment we spend in those environments reinforces powerful aspects of the white racial frame, including a limited worldview, a reliance on deeply problematic depictions of people of color, comfort in segregation with no sense that there might be value in knowing people of color, and internalized superiority. In turn, our capacity to engage constructively across racial lines becomes profoundly limited.

To illustrate an early lesson in white racial framing, imagine that a white mother and her white child are in the grocery store. The child sees a black man and shouts out, "Mommy, that man's skin is black!" Several people, including the black man, turn to look. How do you imagine the mother would respond? Most people would immediately put their finger to their mouth and say, "Shush!" When white people are asked what the mother might be feeling, most agree that she is likely to feel anxiety, tension, and embarrassment. Indeed, many of us have had similar experiences wherein the message was clear: we should not talk openly about race.

When I use this example with my students, sometimes a student will say that the mother is just teaching her child to be polite. In other words, naming this man's race would be impolite. But why? What is shameful about being black—so shameful that we should pretend that we don't notice?[31] The mother's reaction would probably be the same if the man had a visible disability of some kind or was obese. But if the child had seen a white person and shouted out, "Mommy, that man's skin is white!" it is unlikely that the mother would feel the same anxiety, tension, and embarrassment that would have accompanied the first statement.

Now imagine that the child had shouted out how handsome the man was, or how strong. These statements would probably be met with chuckles and smiles. The child would not likely be shushed, because we consider these statements compliments.

The example of a child publicly calling out a black man's race and embarrassing the mother illustrates several aspects of white children's racial socialization. First, children learn that it is taboo to openly talk about race. Second, they learn that people should pretend not to notice undesirable aspects that define some people as less valuable than others (a large birthmark on someone's face, a person using a wheelchair). These lessons manifest themselves later in life, when white adults drop their voices before naming the race of someone who isn't white (and especially so if the race being named is *black*), as if blackness were shameful or the word itself were impolite. If we add all the comments we make about people of color privately, when we are less careful, we may begin to recognize how white children are taught to navigate race.

CHAPTER 3

RACISM AFTER THE CIVIL RIGHTS MOVEMENT

"Children today are so open. When the old folks die off, we will finally be free of racism."

"I grew up in a small rural community, so I was very sheltered. I didn't learn anything about racism."

"I judge people by what they do, not who they are."

"I don't see color; I see people."

"We are all red under the skin."

"I marched in the sixties."

New racism is a term coined by film professor Martin Barker to capture the ways in which racism has adapted over time so that modern norms, policies, and practices result in similar racial outcomes as those in the past, while not appearing to be explicitly racist.[1] Sociologist Eduardo Bonilla-Silva captures this dynamic in the title of his book *Racism Without Racists: Color-Blind Racism and the Persistence of Racial Inequality in America*.[2] He says that though virtually no one claims to be racist anymore, racism still exists. How is that possible? Racism can still exist because it is highly adaptive. Because of this adaptability, we must be able to identify how it changes over time. For example, after a white nationalist march and the murder of a counter-protester, the president of the United States said that there are "very fine people on both sides." This comment would have been unthinkable from a high-ranking public official just a few years ago. Yet if we asked the president if he was a racist, I am confident that he would reply with a resounding no (in fact, he recently stated that he was "the least racist" person one could ever meet). In this chapter, I review various ways that racism has adapted over time to continue to produce racial disparity while it exempts virtually all white people from any involvement in, or benefit from, racism.

All systems of oppression are adaptive; they can withstand and adjust to challenges and still maintain inequality. Take, for instance, the federal recognition of same-sex marriage and accommodations for people with disabilities. While the overall systems of heterosexism and ableism are still with us, they have adapted in limited ways. These adaptations are held up as reassurance to those who fought long and hard for a particular change that equality has now been achieved. These milestones—such as the recognition of same-sex marriage, the passage of the Americans with Disabilities Act, Title 9, the election of Barack Obama—are, of course, significant and worthy of celebration. But systems of oppression are deeply rooted and not overcome with the simple passage of legislation. Advances are also tenuous, as we can see in recent challenges to the rights of LGBTQI (lesbian, gay, bisexual, transgender, queer or questioning, and intersex) people. Systems of oppression are not completely inflexible. But they are far less flexible than popular ideology would acknowledge, and the collective impact of the inequitable distribution of resources continues across history.

COLOR-BLIND RACISM

What is termed color-blind racism is an example of racism's ability to adapt to cultural changes.[3] According to this ideology, if we pretend not to notice race, then there can be no racism. The idea is based on a line from the famous "I Have a Dream" speech given by Dr. Martin Luther King in 1963 during the March on Washington for Jobs and Freedom.

At the time of King's speech, it was much more socially acceptable for white people to admit to their racial prejudices and belief in white racial superiority. But many white people had never witnessed the kind of violence to which blacks were subjected. Because the struggle for civil rights was televised, whites across the nation watched in horror as black men, women, and children were attacked by police dogs and fire hoses during peaceful protests and beaten and dragged away from lunch counters. Once the Civil Rights Act of 1964 was passed (a landmark civil rights and US labor law that outlaws discrimination based on race, color, religion, sex, or national origin), it was less acceptable for white people to admit to racial prejudice; they did not want to be associated with the racist acts they had witnessed on television (in addition to the fact that discrimination was now illegal). One line of King's speech in particular—that one day he might be judged by the content of his character and not the color of his skin—was seized upon by the white public because the words were seen to provide a simple and immediate solution to racial tensions: pretend that we don't see race, and racism will end. Color blindness was now promoted as the remedy for racism, with white people insisting that they didn't see race or, if they did, that it had no meaning to them.

Clearly, the civil rights movement didn't end racism; nor have claims of color blindness. But reducing King's work to this simplistic idea illustrates how movements for social change are co-opted, stripped of their initial challenge, and used against the very cause from which they originated. For example, a common response in the name of color blindness is to declare that an individual who says that race matters is the one who is racist. In other words, it is racist to acknowledge race.

Consider color-blind ideology from the perspective of a person of color. An example I often share occurred when I was co-leading a workshop with an African American man. A white participant said to him, "I don't see race; I don't see you as black." My co-trainer's response was, "Then how will you see racism?" He then explained to her that he was black, he was confident that she could see this, and that his race meant that he had a very different experience in life than she did. If she were ever going to understand or challenge racism, she would need to acknowledge this difference. Pretending that she did not notice that he was black was not helpful to him in any way, as it denied his reality—indeed, it refused his reality—and kept hers insular and unchallenged. This pretense that she did not notice his race assumed that he was "just like her," and in so doing, she projected her reality onto him. For example, I feel welcome at work so you must too; I have never felt that my race mattered, so you must feel that yours doesn't either. But of course, we do see the race of other people, and race holds deep social meaning for us.

We might think of conscious racial awareness as the tip of an iceberg, the superficial aspects of our racial socialization: our intentions (always good!) and what we are supposed to acknowledge seeing (nothing!). Meanwhile, under the surface is the massive depth of racist socialization: messages, beliefs, images, associations, internalized superiority and entitlement, perceptions, and emotions. Color-blind ideology makes it difficult for us to address these unconscious beliefs. While the idea of color blindness may have started out as a well-intentioned strategy for interrupting racism, in practice it has served to deny the reality of racism and thus hold it in place.

Racial bias is largely unconscious, and herein lies the deepest challenge—the defensiveness that ensues upon any suggestion of racial bias.[4] This defensiveness is classic white fragility because it protects our racial bias while simultaneously affirming our identities as open-minded. Yes, it's uncomfortable to be confronted with an aspect of ourselves that we don't like, but we can't change what we refuse to see.

Countless studies show empirically that people of color are discriminated against in the workplace.[5] Imagine you had empirical evidence that your coworker was unintentionally discriminating against people of color during the hiring process. Given your belief in equality, you would probably think that it was imperative to inform the person so that he or she could stop. You pointed this discrimination out in the most diplomatic way possible. Still, what do you think your colleague's response would be? Would you hear gratitude that you had brought that fact to the person's attention? Probably not. More likely, your co-worker would respond with hurt, anger, and defensiveness, insisting that he or she had not racially discriminated but had chosen the most qualified candidates. And the individual would sincerely believe that this was true, even though you had empirical evidence that it was not. This defensiveness is rooted in the false but widespread belief that racial discrimination can only be intentional. Our lack of understanding about implicit bias leads to aversive racism.

AVERSIVE RACISM

Aversive racism is a manifestation of racism that well-intentioned people who see themselves as educated and progressive are more likely to exhibit.[6] It exists under the surface of consciousness because it conflicts with consciously held beliefs of racial equality and justice. Aversive racism is a subtle but insidious form, as aversive racists enact racism in ways that allow them to maintain a positive self-image (e.g., "I have lots of friends of color"; "I judge people by the content of their character, not the color of their skin").

Whites enact racism while maintaining a positive self-image in many ways:

- Rationalizing racial segregation as unfortunate but necessary to access "good schools"
- Rationalizing that our workplaces are virtually all white because people of color just don't apply
- Avoiding direct racial language and using racially coded terms such as *urban, underprivileged, diverse, sketchy*, and *good neighborhoods*

- Denying that we have few cross-racial relationships by proclaiming how diverse our community or workplace is
- Attributing inequality between whites and people of color to causes other than racism

Consider a conversation I had with a white friend. She was telling me about a (white) couple she knew who had just moved to New Orleans and bought a house for a mere twenty-five thousand dollars. "Of course," she immediately added, "they also had to buy a gun, and Joan is afraid to leave the house." I immediately knew they had bought a home in a black neighborhood. This was a moment of white racial bonding between this couple who shared the story of racial danger and my friend, and then between my friend and me, as she repeated the story. Through this tale, the four of us fortified familiar images of the horror of black space and drew boundaries between "us" and "them" without ever having to directly name race or openly express our disdain for black space.

Notice that the need for a gun is a key part of this story—it would not have the degree of social capital it holds if the emphasis were on the price of the house alone. Rather, the story's emotional power rests on why a house would be that cheap—because it is in a black neighborhood where white people literally might not get out alive. Yet while very negative and stereotypical representations of blacks were reinforced in that exchange, not naming race provided plausible deniability. In fact, in preparing to share this incident, I texted my friend and asked her the name of the city her friends had moved to. I also wanted to confirm my assumption that she was talking about a black neighborhood. I share the text exchange here:

"Hey, what city did you say your friends had bought a house in for $25,000?"
"New Orleans. They said they live in a very bad neighborhood and they each have to have a gun to protect themselves. I wouldn't pay 5 cents for that neighborhood."
"I assume it's a black neighborhood?"

"Yes. You get what you pay for. I'd rather pay $500,000 and live somewhere where I wasn't afraid."

"I wasn't asking because I want to live there. I'm writing about this in my book, the way that white people talk about race without ever coming out and talking about race."

"I wouldn't want you to live there it's too far away from me!"

Notice that when I simply ask what city the house is in, she repeats the story about the neighborhood being so bad that her friends need guns. When I ask if the neighborhood is black, she is comfortable confirming that it is. But when I tell her that I am interested in how whites talk about race without talking about race, she switches the narrative. Now her concern is about not wanting me to live so far away. This is a classic example of aversive racism: holding deep racial disdain that surfaces in daily discourse but not being able to admit it because the disdain conflicts with our self-image and professed beliefs.

Readers may be asking themselves, "But if the neighborhood is really dangerous, why is acknowledging this danger a sign of racism?" Research in implicit bias has shown that perceptions of criminal activity are influenced by race. White people will perceive danger simply by the presence of black people; we cannot trust our perceptions when it comes to race and crime.[7] But regardless of whether the neighborhood is actually more or less dangerous than other neighborhoods, what is salient about this exchange is how it functions racially and what that means for the white people engaged in it. For my friend and me, this conversation did not increase our awareness of the danger of some specific neighborhood. Rather, the exchange reinforced our fundamental beliefs about black people. Toni Morrison uses the term *race talk* to capture "the explicit insertion into everyday life of racial signs and symbols that have no meaning other than positioning African Americans into the lowest level of the racial hierarchy."[8] Casual race talk is a key component of white racial framing because it accomplishes the interconnected goals of elevating whites while demeaning people of color; race talk always implies a racial "us" and "them."

Consider an experience I had with aversive racism. My last academic position was in a state I had never been to before my interview. Throughout the three days of interviewing, other white people warned me not to buy a home in Springfield or Holyoke if I took the position, especially if I had children. While no one openly named race, the racial coding was not lost on me. I now knew where the people of color were concentrated in the area. At the same time, because no one directly mentioned race, we could all deny that this was what we were actually talking about. Returning to my hotel room the first night, I looked up the demographics. Sure enough, Springfield and Holyoke had significantly high populations, close to 50 percent, of black and brown people. Starting on day one of my visit, my fellow whites had communicated the racial boundaries to me.[9]

My teacher-education students also engaged in race talk—reinforcing the boundaries between "us" and "them" while positioning us as superior. They engaged in race talk when they expressed fear about being placed in "dangerous" neighborhoods while describing their hometowns as "sheltered." These depictions are relentlessly strengthened by news stories that position violent crime committed in primarily white suburban communities as shocking, yet claiming that one has grown up in a sheltered environment raises a question that begs to be answered: "Sheltered from what and in contrast to whom?" If we grow up in environments with few if any people of color, are we not in fact less sheltered from racist conditioning because we have to rely on narrow and repetitive media representations, jokes, omissions, and warnings for our understanding of people of color?

Conversely, positioning white spaces as sheltered and those who are raised in them as racially innocent taps into classic narratives of people of color as *not* innocent. Racist images and resultant white fears can be found at all levels of society, and myriad studies demonstrate that whites believe that people of color (and blacks in particular) are dangerous.[10]

Whites rarely consider how sheltered and safe their spaces may be from the perspective of people of color (e.g., Trayvon Martin's experience in a gated white community). Because it reverses the actual direction of racial danger, this narrative may be one of the most pernicious.

When you consider the moral judgment we make about people we deem as racist in our society, the need to deny our own racism—even to ourselves—makes sense. We believe we are superior at a deeply internalized level and act on this belief in the practice of our lives, but we must deny this belief to fit into society and maintain our self-identity as good, moral people. Unfortunately, aversive racism only protects racism, because we can't challenge our racial filters if we can't consider the possibility that we have them. Of course, some whites explicitly avow racism. We might consider these whites actually more aware of, and honest about, their biases than those of us who consider ourselves open-minded yet who have rarely thought critically about the biases we inevitably hold or how we may be expressing them.

CULTURAL RACISM

The body of research about children and race demonstrates that white children develop a sense of white superiority as early as preschool.[11] This early start shouldn't be surprising, as society sends constant messages that to be white is better than to be a person of color.

Despite the claims of many white young adults that racism is in the past and that they were taught to see everyone as equal, research shows otherwise. For example, polls sponsored by MTV in 2014 show that millennials profess more tolerance and a deeper commitment to equality and fairness than previous generations did.[12] At the same time, millennials are committed to an ideal of color blindness that leaves them uncomfortable with, and confused about, race and opposed to measures to reduce racial inequality. Perhaps most significantly, 41 percent of white millennials believe that government pays too much attention to minorities, and 48 percent believe that discrimination against whites is as big a problem as discrimination against people of color. Many in this generation claim that the election of Barack Obama as president shows that we are postracial. These polls were conducted before the presidency of Donald Trump, but as his election has made clear, we are far from being postracial.

Another significant study that was based on the practices of millennials rather than their claims was conducted by sociologists Leslie Picca and Joe Feagin.[13] They asked 626 white college students at twenty-eight colleges across the United States to keep journals and record every instance of racial issues, racial images, and racial understanding that they observed or were part of for six to eight weeks. The students recorded more than seventy-five hundred accounts of blatantly racist comments and actions by the white people in their lives (friends, families, acquaintances, strangers). These accounts come from the generation most likely to claim they were taught to see everyone as equal—those who grew up in the age of color-blind ideology after the civil rights movement. Picca and Feagin's study provides empirical evidence that racism continues to be explicitly expressed by whites, even those who are young and profess to be progressive. Consider these examples from their study:

> "As I sit in a room with a bunch of frat guys, Phil walks in chanting 'rotchie, rotchie, rotchie!!' I ask . . . what that term means and I am answered with a giggle and a quick 'it's slang for nigger, like niggerotchie.' . . ." [Eileen]

> "Robby was there telling a joke. . . . He glanced to see if anyone was around. He starts, 'A black man, a Latin man, and a white guy find a magical lamp on the beach [racist joke ensues].' I thought it was pretty funny and I wasn't the only one. But, I'm glad he waited till no one was around to tell it. If you didn't know Robby you might misunderstand." [Ashley][14]

Several common dynamics are illustrated in the thousands of examples Picca and Feagin collected. The first is how much explicit racism young people are exposed to and participate in. The second is the idea that if someone is a good person, he or she cannot be racist, as demonstrated in the student's note that if someone overheard, the person might "misunderstand" Robby. This sort of racism makes for a very challenging dynamic in which whites are operating under the false assumption that we can't simultaneously be good people and participate in racism, at the same time that we are dishonest about what we really think and do regarding people of color.

The study also reveals a consistent pattern in how these comments and actions were expressed. The majority of incidents occurred in what the researchers describe as the *backstage*—in all-white company. Further, they found that whites involved in these incidents most often played predictable roles. Typically, there was a protagonist who initiated the racist act, a cheerleader who encouraged it through laughter or agreement, the spectators who stood in silence, and (very rarely) a dissenter who objected. Virtually all dissenters were subjected to a form of peer pressure in which they were told that it was only a joke and that they should lighten up.

The researchers document that in front-stage settings (those in which people of color were present), the white students displayed a range of racially conscious behaviors, including the following:

- Acting overly nice
- Avoiding contact (e.g., crossing a street or not going to a particular bar or club)
- Mimicking "black mannerisms and speech"
- Being careful not to use racial terms or labels
- Using code words to talk negatively about people of color
- Occasional violence directed at people of color

In backstage settings, where people of color were not present, white students often used humor to reinforce racial stereotypes about people of color, particularly blacks. Picca and Feagin argue that the purpose of these backstage performances is to create white solidarity and to reinforce the ideology of white and male supremacy. This behavior keeps racism circulating, albeit in less formal but perhaps more powerful ways than in the past. Today we have a cultural norm that insists we hide our racism from people of color and deny it among ourselves, but not that we actually challenge it. In fact, we are socially penalized for challenging racism.

I am often asked if I think the younger generation is less racist. No, I don't. In some ways, racism's adaptations over time are more sinister than concrete rules such as Jim Crow. The adaptations produce the same outcome (people of color are blocked from moving forward) but have been put in place by a dominant white society that won't or can't admit to its beliefs. This intransigence results in another pillar of white fragility: the refusal to know.

CHAPTER 4

HOW DOES RACE SHAPE THE LIVES OF WHITE PEOPLE?

*White People: I don't want you to understand me
better; I want you to understand yourselves. Your
survival has never depended on your knowledge of
white culture. In fact, it's required your ignorance.*

—Ijeoma Oluo

To understand how white people become so difficult in conversations about race, we need to understand the underlying foundation of white fragility: how being white shapes our perspectives, experiences, and responses. Every aspect of being white discussed in this chapter is shared by virtually all white people in the Western context generally and the US context specifically. At the same time, no person of color in this context can make these same claims.

BELONGING

I was born into a culture in which I belonged, racially. Indeed, the forces of racism were shaping me even before I took my first breath. If I were born in a hospital, regardless of the decade in which I was born, any hospital would be open to me because my parents were white. If my parents attended a childbirth preparation class, the instructor was most likely white, the videos they watched in class most likely depicted white people, and their fellow classmates with whom they built connections and community were also most likely white. When my parents read their birthing manuals and other written materials, the pictures most likely depicted primarily white mothers and fathers, doctors and nurses. If they took a parenting class, the theories and models of child development were based on white racial identity. The doctors and nurses attending my birth were in all likelihood white. Although my parents may have been anxious about the birth process, they did not have to worry about how they would be treated by the hospital staff because of their race. The years of research demonstrating racial discrimination in health care assure me that my parents were more likely to have been treated well by hospital personnel and to receive a higher caliber of care than would people of color.[1]

Conversely, the people who cleaned my mother's hospital room, did the laundry, cooked and cleaned in the cafeteria, and maintained the facilities were most likely people of color. The very context in which I entered the world was organized hierarchically by race. Based on this hierarchy, we could predict whether I would survive my birth based on my race.

As I move through my daily life, my race is unremarkable. I belong when I turn on the TV, read best-selling novels, and watch blockbuster movies. I belong when I walk past the magazine racks at the grocery store or drive past billboards. I belong when I see the overwhelming number of white people on lists of the "Most Beautiful." I may feel inadequate in light of my age or weight, but I will belong racially. For example, in 2017, singer Rhianna introduced a makeup line for women of all skin colors. Gratitude from women of color poured in. Many of their tweets included the exclamation "Finally!"[2] These are tweets I have never needed to send.

I belong when I look at my teachers, counselors, and classmates. I belong when I learn about the history of my country throughout the year and when I am shown its heroes and heroines—George Washington, Thomas Jefferson, Abraham Lincoln, Robert E. Lee, Amelia Earhart, Susan B. Anthony, John Glenn, Sally Ride, and Louisa May

Alcott.[3] I belong when I look through my textbooks and at the pictures on my classroom walls. I belong when I speak to my children's teachers, when I talk to their camp counselors, when I consult with their doctors and dentists. No matter how I might explain why all these representations are overwhelmingly white, they still shape my identity and worldview.

In virtually every situation or context deemed normal, neutral or prestigious in society, I belong racially. This belonging is a deep and ever-present feeling that has always been with me. Belonging has settled deep into my consciousness; it shapes my daily thoughts and concerns, what I reach for in life, and what I expect to find. The experience of belonging is so natural that I do not have to think about it. The rare moments in which I don't belong racially come as a surprise—a surprise that I can either enjoy for its novelty or easily avoid if I find it unsettling.

For example, I was invited to the retirement party of a white friend. The party was a pot-luck picnic held in a public park. As I walked down the slope toward the picnic shelters, I noticed two parties going on side by side. One gathering was primarily composed of white people, and the other appeared to be all black people. I experienced a sense of disequilibrium as I approached and had to choose which party was my friend's. I felt a mild sense of anxiety as I considered that I might have to enter the all-black group, then mild relief as I realized that my friend was in the other group. This relief was amplified as I thought that I might have mistakenly walked over to the black party! All these thoughts and feelings happened in just a few seconds, but they were a rare moment of racial self-awareness. The mere possibility that I might have to experience not belonging racially was enough to raise racial discomfort.

It is rare for me to experience a sense of not belonging racially, and these are usually very temporary, easily avoidable situations. Indeed, throughout my life, I have been warned that I should avoid situations in which I might be a racial minority. These situations are often presented as scary, dangerous, or "sketchy." Yet if the environment or situation is viewed as good, nice, or valuable, I can be confident that as a white person, I will be seen as racially belonging there.

FREEDOM FROM THE BURDEN OF RACE

Because I haven't been socialized to see myself or to be seen by other whites in racial terms, I don't carry the psychic weight of race; I don't have to worry about how others feel about my race. Nor do I worry that my race will be held against me. While I may feel unease in an upper-class environment, I will take for granted that I belong racially in these settings. I certainly will not be the only white person there, unless the event is specifically organized by, or celebrating, people of color. George Zimmerman would not have stopped me as I walked through a gated suburban neighborhood.

Patrick Rosal writes poignantly about the pain of being mistaken for the help at a black-tie event celebrating National Book Award winners.[4] I have witnessed this assumption of servitude many times as I checked into hotels with colleagues of color. I have made this assumption myself when I have been unable to hide my surprise that the black man is the school principal or when I ask a Latinx woman kneeling in her garden if this is her home.

As I consider career choices I will have countless role models across a vast array of fields. When I apply for a job, virtually anyone in a position to hire me will share my race. And although I may encounter a token person of color during the hiring process, if I am not specifically applying to an organization founded by people of color, the majority of those I interact with will share my race. Once hired, I won't have to deal with my coworkers' resentment that I only got the job because I am white; I am assumed to be the most qualified.[5] If there are people of color in the organization who resent my hire, I can easily dismiss them and rest assured that their feelings won't carry much weight. If resentment from employees of color does manage to come to my attention, I can find copious validation and other support from my white coworkers, who will reassure me that our colleagues of color are the ones who are biased. With race as a nonissue, I can focus on my work and productivity and be seen as a team player. This is yet another example of the concept of whiteness as property discussed earlier: whiteness has psychological advantages that translate into material returns.

As I move through my day, racism just isn't my problem. While I am aware that race has been used unfairly against people of color, I haven't been taught to see this problem as any responsibility of mine; as long as I personally haven't done anything I am aware of, racism is a nonissue. This freedom from responsibility gives me a level of racial relaxation and emotional and intellectual space that people of color are not afforded as they move through their day. They don't lack these benefits just because they are members of a numerical minority and I am not (white men are a numerical minority). People of color lack these benefits because they are racialized within a culture of white supremacy—a culture in which they are seen as inferior, if they are seen at all.

Raised in a culture of white supremacy, I exude a deeply internalized assumption of racial superiority. Having to navigate white people's internalized assumption of racial superiority is a great psychic drain for people of color, but I have no need to concern myself with that.

FREEDOM OF MOVEMENT

I am free to move in virtually any space seen as normal, neutral, or valuable. While I might worry about my class status in some settings, for example, when attending a "high-society" event such as a museum opening or an art auction, I will not have to worry about my race. In fact, my race will work in my favor in these settings, granting me the initial benefit of the doubt that I belong there.[6] I also will certainly not be the only white person there, unless the event is specifically organized by, or celebrating, people of color.

In the early years of my career as a workplace diversity trainer, I co-led the workshops with Deborah, an African American woman. After a particularly grueling travel schedule, I proposed that we get away for a relaxing weekend and suggested Lake Coeur d'Alene in Idaho. Deborah laughed at the suggestion and let me know that visiting northern Idaho did not sound like a relaxing weekend for her. Besides being a very small town, Lake Coeur d'Alene is near Hayden Lake, where the Aryan Nation was building a compound.[7] Although not all people who live in the area are avowed white nationalists, the knowledge that some people might be part of this openly racist group was terrifying for Deborah. Even if there were no organized white nationalist encampments in the area, Deborah did not want to be isolated in a virtually all-white environment and have to interact with white people who may have never met a black person before. Yet as a white person, I did not have to consider any of this; all places I perceive as beautiful are open to me racially, and my expectation is that I will have a pleasant and relaxing experience there.

JUST PEOPLE

Another way that my life has been shaped by being white is that my race is held up as the norm for humanity. Whites are "just people"—our race is rarely if ever named. Think about how often white people mention the race of a person if they are not white: my black friend, the Asian woman. I enjoy young adult literature but am taken aback by how consistently the race of characters of color is named and how only those characters' races are named.

To use an example from school, consider the writers we are all expected to read; the list usually includes Ernest Hemingway, John Steinbeck, Charles Dickens, Fyodor Dostoevsky, Mark Twain, Jane Austen, and William Shakespeare. These writers are seen as representing the universal human experience, and we read them precisely because they are presumed to be able to speak to us all. Now consider the writers we turn to during events promoting diversity—events such as Multicultural Authors Week and Black History Month. These writers usually include Maya Angelou, Toni Morrison, James Baldwin, Amy Tan, and Sandra Cisneros. We go to these writers for the black or Asian perspective; Toni Morrison is always seen as a black writer, not just a writer. But when we are not looking for the black or Asian perspective, we return to white writers, reinforcing the idea of whites as just human, and people of color as particular kinds (racialized) of humans. This also allows white (male) writers to be seen as not having an agenda or any particular perspective, while racialized (and gendered) writers do.

Virtually any representation of *human* is based on white people's norms and images—"flesh-colored" makeup, standard emoji, depictions of Adam and Eve, Jesus and Mary, educational models of the human body with white skin and blue eyes.[8] Take, for example, a photograph that was circulated widely and featured in the *Daily Mail*. The photo of a blond, blue-eyed white woman is captioned "What Would a Scientifically Perfect Face Look Like?" Below the image is the question "Is this the perfect face?"[9] This one example illustrates several concepts discussed thus far: the white racial frame, whiteness as the human norm, whiteness as ideal beauty, and whiteness as naturally superior. Not only is the idea behind the claim racially problematic in its own right, but it rests on and reinforces the backdrop of an earlier era of scientific racism.

Consider models for child development and its stages, and how our culture talks about children as a collective group. Theorists present human development as if it were universal. Occasionally, we may distinguish between boys and girls, but even then, the categories are presumed to include all boys or all girls. Now consider all the dynamics I have discussed thus far. Is an Asian or an Indigenous child's development the same as a white child's within the context of white supremacy?

WHITE SOLIDARITY

White solidarity is the unspoken agreement among whites to protect white advantage and not cause another white person to feel racial discomfort by confronting them when they say or do something racially problematic. Educational researcher Christine Sleeter describes this solidarity as white "racial bonding." She observes that when whites interact, they affirm "a common stance on race-related issues, legitimating particular interpretations of groups of color, and drawing conspiratorial we-they boundaries."[10] White solidarity requires both silence about anything that exposes the advantages of the white position and tacit agreement to remain racially united in the protection of white supremacy. To break white solidarity is to break rank.

We see white solidarity at the dinner table, at parties, and in work settings. Many of us can relate to the big family dinner at which Uncle Bob says something racially offensive. Everyone cringes but no one challenges him because nobody wants to ruin the dinner. Or the party where someone tells a racist joke but we keep silent because we don't want to be accused of being too politically correct and be told to lighten up. In the workplace, we avoid naming racism for the same reasons, in addition to wanting to be seen as a team player and to avoid anything that may jeopardize our career advancement. All these familiar scenarios are examples of white solidarity. (Why speaking up about racism would ruin the ambiance or threaten our career advancement is something we might want to talk about.)

The very real consequences of breaking white solidarity play a fundamental role in maintaining white supremacy. We do indeed risk censure and other penalties from our fellow whites. We might be accused of being politically correct or might be perceived as angry, humorless, combative, and not suited to go far in an organization. In my own life, these penalties have worked as a form of social coercion. Seeking to avoid conflict and wanting to be liked, I have chosen silence all too often.

Conversely, when I kept quiet about racism, I was rewarded with social capital such as being seen as fun, cooperative, and a team player. Notice that within a white supremacist society, I am rewarded for not interrupting racism and punished in a range of ways—big and small— when I do. I can justify my silence by telling myself that at least I am not the one who made the joke and that therefore I am not at fault. But my silence is not benign because it protects and maintains the racial hierarchy and my place within it. Each uninterrupted joke furthers the circulation of racism through the culture, and the ability for the joke to circulate depends on my complicity.

People of color certainly experience white solidarity as a form of racism, wherein we fail to hold each other accountable, to challenge racism when we see it, or to support people of color in the struggle for racial justice.

THE GOOD OLD DAYS

As a white person, I can openly and unabashedly reminisce about "the good old days." Romanticized recollections of the past and calls for a return to former ways are a function of white privilege, which manifests itself in the ability to remain oblivious to our racial history. Claiming that the past was socially better than the present is also a hallmark of white supremacy. Consider any period in the past from the perspective of people of color: 246 years of brutal enslavement; the rape of black women for the pleasure of white men and to produce more enslaved workers; the selling off of black children; the attempted genocide of Indigenous people, Indian removal acts, and reservations; indentured servitude, lynching, and mob violence; sharecropping; Chinese exclusion laws; Japanese American internment; Jim Crow laws of mandatory segregation; black codes; bans on black jury service; bans on voting; imprisoning people for unpaid work; medical sterilization and experimentation; employment discrimination; educational discrimination; inferior schools; biased laws and policing practices; redlining and subprime mortgages; mass incarceration; racist media representations; cultural erasures, attacks, and mockery; and untold and perverted historical accounts, and you can see how a romanticized past is strictly a white construct. But it is a powerful construct because it calls out to a deeply internalized sense of superiority and entitlement and the sense that any advancement for people of color is an encroachment on this entitlement.

The past was great for white people (and white men in particular) because their positions went largely unchallenged. In understanding the power of white fragility, we have to notice that the mere questioning of those positions triggered the white fragility that Trump capitalized on. There has been no actual loss of power for the white elite, who have always controlled our institutions and continue to do so by a very wide margin. Of the fifty richest people on earth, twenty-nine are American.

Of these twenty-nine, all are white, and all but two are men (Lauren Jobs inherited her husband's wealth, and Alice Walton her father's).

Similarly, the white working class has always held the top positions within blue-collar fields (the overseers, labor leaders, and fire and police chiefs). And although globalization and the erosion of workers' rights has had a profound impact on the white working class, white fragility enabled the white elite to direct the white working class's resentment toward people of color. The resentment is clearly misdirected, given that the people who control the economy and who have managed to concentrate more wealth into fewer (white) hands than ever before in human history are the white elite.

Consider this data on the distribution of wealth:

- Since 2015, the richest 1 percent has owned more wealth than the rest of the planet owns.[11]
- Eight men own the same amount of wealth as do the poorest half of the world.
- The incomes of the poorest 10 percent of people increased by less than three dollars a year between 1988 and 2011, while the incomes of the richest 1 percent increased 182 times as much.
- In Bloomberg's daily ranking of the world's five hundred richest people, the world's wealthiest three (Bill Gates, Warren Buffet, and Jeff Bezos), all white American men, have total net worths of $85 billion, $79 billion, and $73 billion, respectively.[12] By comparison, the 2015 gross domestic product of Sri Lanka was $82 billion; Luxembourg $58 billion; and Iceland, $16 billion.[13]
- Of the world's ten richest people, nine are white men.[14]
- In 2015–2016, the world's ten biggest corporations together had revenue greater than that of the government revenues of 180 countries combined.
- In the US, over the last thirty years, the growth in the incomes of the bottom 50 percent has been zero, whereas incomes of the top 1 percent have grown by 300 percent.

The call to Make America Great Again worked powerfully in service of the racial manipulation of white people, diverting blame away from the white elite and toward various peoples of color—for example, undocumented workers, immigrants, and the Chinese—for the current conditions of the white working class.

The romanticized "traditional" family values of the past are also racially problematic. White families fled from cities to the suburbs to escape the influx of people of color, a process sociologists term *white flight*. They wrote covenants to keep schools and neighborhoods segregated and forbade cross-racial dating.

Consider the extreme resistance to busing and other forms of school integration from white parents. In the landmark Supreme Court decision *Brown v. Board of Education*, the court ruled that separate was inherently unequal and that schools needed to desegregate "with all deliberate speed." Busing children from one neighborhood into a school in another to account for residential segregation became a major strategy of desegregation (notably, white children were generally not bused into predominately black schools; instead, black children endured long bus rides to attend predominately white schools). Regina Williams, a black student from Roxbury, Massachusetts, was bused into a school in South Boston. She described her first day in a formerly all-white school as "like a war zone." School officials, politicians, the courts, and the media gave precedence to the desires of white parents who overwhelmingly and vehemently opposed school desegregation. It has not been African Americans who resist integration efforts; it has always been whites.[15] The practice of our lives as a white collective has rarely been in alignment with the values we profess.

At the minimum, this idealization of the past is another example of white experiences and perceptions positioned as universal. How might this nostalgia sound to any person of color who is aware of this country's history? The ability to erase this racial history and actually believe that the past was better than the present "for everybody" has inculcated a false consciousness for me personally and as a national citizen.

WHITE RACIAL INNOCENCE

Because we are not raised to see ourselves in racial terms or to see white space as racialized space, we position ourselves as innocent of race. On countless occasions, I have heard white people claim that because they grew up in segregation, they were sheltered from race. At the same time, we turn to people of color, who may also have grown up in racially segregated spaces (because of decades of de jure and de facto policies that blocked them from moving into white neighborhoods) to learn about racism. But why aren't people of color who grew up in segregation also innocent of race? I ask my readers to reflect deeply on the idea that white segregation is racially innocent.

Because people of color are not seen as racially innocent, they are expected to speak to issues of race (but must do so on white terms). This idea—that racism is not a white problem—enables us to sit back and let people of color take very real risks of invalidation and retaliation as they share their experiences. But we are not required to take similar cross-racial risks. They—not we—have race, and thus they are the holders of racial knowledge. In this way, we position ourselves as standing outside hierarchical social relations.

White flight may be seen as another aspect of white racial innocence, as it is often justified by beliefs that people of color (again, especially black people) are more prone to crime and that if "too many" black people move into a neighborhood, crime will increase, home values will go down, and the neighborhood will deteriorate. For example, in a study of race and perceptions of crime conducted by sociologists Heather Johnson and Thomas Shapiro, white families consistently discussed fear of crime and associated crime with people of color. In their minds, the more people of color in an area (specifically, blacks and Latinos), the more dangerous the area was perceived to be. Research matching census data and police department crime statistics show that this association does not hold, but these statistics do not quell white fears. For most whites, the percentage of young men of color in a neighborhood is directly correlated with perceptions of the neighborhood crime level.[16]

Deeply held white associations of black people with crime distort reality and the actual direction of danger that has historically existed between whites and blacks. The vast history of extensive and brutal explicit violence perpetrated by whites and their ideological rationalizations are all trivialized through white claims of racial innocence. The power we now wield and have wielded for centuries is thus obscured.

It has been well documented that blacks and Latinos are stopped by police more often than whites are for the same activities and that they receive harsher sentences than whites do for the same crimes. Research has also shown that a major reason for this racial disparity can be attributed to the beliefs held by judges and others about the cause of the criminal behavior.[17] For example, the criminal behavior of white juveniles is often seen as caused by external factors—the youth comes from a single-parent home, is having a hard time right now, just happened to be at the wrong place at the wrong time, or was bullied at school. Attributing the cause of the action to external factors lessens the person's responsibility and classifies the person as a victim him or herself. But black and Latinx youth are not afforded this same compassion.

When black and Latinx youth go before a judge, the cause of the crime is more often attributed to something internal to the person—the youth is naturally more prone to crime, is more animalistic, and has less capacity for remorse (similarly, a 2016 study found that half of a sample of medical students and residents believe that blacks feel less pain[18]). Whites continually receive the benefit of the doubt not granted to people of color—our race alone helps establish our innocence.

For those of us who work to raise the racial consciousness of whites, simply getting whites to acknowledge that our race gives us advantages is a major effort. The defensiveness, denial, and resistance are deep. But acknowledging advantage is only a first step, and this acknowledgment can be used in a way that renders it meaningless and allows us white people to exempt ourselves from further responsibility. For example, I have often heard whites dismissively say, "Just because of the color of my skin, I have privilege." Statements like this describe privilege as if it's a fluke—something that just happens to us as we move through life, with no involvement or complicity on our part.

Critical race scholar Zeus Leonardo critiques the concept of white privilege as something white people receive unwittingly. He says that this concept is analogous to suggesting that a person could walk through life with other people stuffing money into his or her pockets without any awareness or consent on the walker's part. Leonardo challenges this conceptualization, which positions white privilege as innocence, by arguing that "for white racial hegemony to saturate everyday life, it has to be secured by a process of domination, or those acts, decisions, and policies that white subjects perpetrate on people of color."[19] Viewing privilege as something that white people are just handed obscures the systematic dimensions of racism that must be actively and passively, consciously and unconsciously, maintained.

The expectation that people of color should teach white people about racism is another aspect of white racial innocence that reinforces several problematic racial assumptions. First, it implies that racism is something that happens to people of color and has nothing to do with us and that we consequently cannot be expected to have any knowledge of it. This framework denies that racism is a relationship in which both groups are involved. By leaving it to people of color to tackle racial issues, we offload the tensions and social dangers of speaking openly onto them. We can ignore the risks ourselves and remain silent on questions of our own culpability.

Second, this request requires nothing of us and reinforces unequal power relations by asking people of color to do our work. There are copious resources available on the subject generated by people of color who are willing to share the information; why haven't we sought it out before this conversation?

Third, the request ignores the historical dimensions of race relations. It disregards how often people of color have indeed tried to tell us what racism is like for them and how often they have been dismissed. To ask people of color to tell us how they experience racism without first building a trusting relationship and being willing to meet them halfway by also being vulnerable shows that we are not racially aware and that this exchange will probably be invalidating for them.

SEGREGATED LIVES

On a television talk show in 1965, James Baldwin responded passionately to a Yale professor's argument that Baldwin always concentrated on color:

> I don't know if white Christians hate Negros or not, but I know that we have a Christian church that is white and a Christian church which is black. I know that the most segregated hour in American life is high noon on Sunday. . . . I don't know whether the labor unions and their bosses really hate me . . . but I know I am not in their unions. I don't know if the real estate lobby is against black people but I know that the real estate lobbyists keep me in the ghetto. I don't know if the Board of Education hates Black people, but I know the textbooks they give my children to read and the schools that we have to go to. Now this is the evidence. You want me to make an act of faith risking . . . my life . . . on some idealism which you assure me exists in America which I have never seen.[20]

Life in the United States is deeply shaped by racial segregation. Of all racial groups, whites are the most likely to choose segregation and are the group most likely to be in the social and economic position to do so.[21] Growing up in segregation (our schools, workplaces, neighborhoods, shopping districts, places of worship, entertainment, social gatherings, and elsewhere) reinforces the message that our experiences and perspectives are the only ones that matter. We don't see people of color around us, and few if any adults acknowledge a lack of racial diversity as a problem. In fact, the classification of which neighborhoods are good and which are bad is always based on race. These assessments may also be based on economic divisions among whites, but if black and Latinx students attend a school in significant numbers (significant in the white mind), whites will perceive the school as bad. If there *are* people of color around us, we are seldom encouraged to build cross-racial friendships.

Segregation is often lessened somewhat for poor urban whites who may live near and have friendships with people of color on the local level because white poverty brings white people into proximity with people of color in a way that suburban and middle-class life does not (except during gentrification, when the mixing is temporary). Urban whites from the lower classes may have more integrated lives on the micro level, but we still receive the message that achievement means moving away from the neighborhoods and schools that illuminate our poverty. Upward mobility is the great class goal in the United States, and the social environment gets tangibly whiter the higher up you climb. Whiter environments, in turn, are seen as the most desirable.

For upwardly mobile whites from the lower classes, reaching toward the most valuable places in society usually means leaving friends and neighbors of color behind. For example, I grew up urban and poor and lived in apartment buildings in crowded rental-based neighborhoods. In my childhood, there were many people of color around me. But I knew that if I was to improve my life, I would not stay in these neighborhoods; upward mobility would take me to whiter spaces, and it has. I did not maintain those early relationships with people of color, and no one who guided me encouraged me to do so. Segregation was still operating in my life at the wider societal level: it dictated what I learned in school, read in books, saw on TV, and learned to value if I wanted to improve my life.

Meritocracy is a precious ideology in the United States, but neighborhoods and schools are demonstrably not equal; they are separate and unequal. Tax bases, school resources, curricula, textbooks, opportunities for extracurricular activities, and the quality of the teaching staff differ widely between school districts. Who is not aware that schools in the United States are vastly unequal? Without white people's interest or effort invested in changing a system that serves them at the expense of others, advantage is passed down from generation to generation. Rather than change these conditions so that public education is equal for all, we allow other people's children to endure conditions that would be unacceptable for our own.

A 2009 study published in the *American Journal of Education* found that while suburban parents, who are mostly white, say they are selecting schools on the basis of test scores, the racial makeup of a school actually plays a larger role in their school decisions. Amy Stuart Wells, a professor of sociology and education at Columbia University's Teachers College, found the same coded language when she studied how white parents choose schools in New York City. She writes, "In a postracial era, we don't have to say it's about race or the color of the kids in the building. . . . We can concentrate poverty and kids of color and then fail to provide the resources to support and sustain those schools, and then we can see a school full of black kids and say, 'Oh, look at their test scores.' It's all very tidy now, this whole system."[22] Readers have no doubt heard schools and neighborhoods discussed in these terms and know that this talk is racially coded; "urban" and "low test scores" are code for "not white" and therefore less desirable.

While many whites see spaces inhabited by more than a few people of color as undesirable and even dangerous, consider another perspective. I have heard countless people of color describe how painful an experience it was to be one of only a few people of color in their schools and neighborhoods. Although many parents of color want the advantages granted by attending predominantly white schools, they also worry about the stress and even the danger they are putting their children in. These parents understand that the predominantly white teaching force has little if any authentic knowledge about children of color and has been socialized (often unconsciously) to see children of color as inferior and even to fear them. Imagine how unsafe white schools, which are so precious to white parents, might appear to parents of color.

The most profound message of racial segregation may be that the absence of people of color from our lives is no real loss. Not one person who loved me, guided me, or taught me ever conveyed that segregation deprived me of anything of value. I could live my entire life without a friend or loved one of color and not see that as a diminishment of my life. In fact, my life trajectory would almost certainly ensure that I had few, if any, people of color in my life. I might meet a few people of color if I played certain sports in school, or if there happened to be one or two persons of color in my class, but when I was outside of that context, I had no proximity to people of color, much less any authentic relationships. Most whites who recall having a friend of color in childhood rarely keep these friendships into adulthood. Yet if my parents had thought it was valuable to have cross-racial relationships, they would have ensured that I had them, even if it took effort—the same effort so many white parents expend to send their children across town so they can attend a better (whiter) school.

Pause for a moment and consider the profundity of this message: we are taught that we lose nothing of value through racial segregation. Consider the message we send to our children—as well as to children of color—when we describe white segregation as good.

In summary, our socialization engenders a common set of racial patterns. These patterns are the foundation of white fragility:

- Preference for racial segregation, and a lack of a sense of loss about segregation
- Lack of understanding about what racism is
- Seeing ourselves as individuals, exempt from the forces of racial socialization
- Failure to understand that we bring our group's history with us, that history matters
- Assuming everyone is having or can have our experience
- Lack of racial humility, and unwillingness to listen
- Dismissing what we don't understand
- Lack of authentic interest in the perspectives of people of color
- Wanting to jump over the hard, personal work and get to "solutions"
- Confusing disagreement with not understanding

- Need to maintain white solidarity, to save face, to look good
- Guilt that paralyzes or allows inaction
- Defensiveness about any suggestion that we are connected to racism
- A focus on intentions over impact

My psychosocial development was inculcated in a white supremacist culture in which I am in the superior group. Telling me to treat everyone the same is not enough to override this socialization; nor is it humanly possible. I was raised in a society that taught me that there was no loss in the absence of people of color—that their absence was a good and desirable thing to be sought and maintained—while simutaneously denying that fact. This attitude has shaped every aspect of my self-identity: my interests and investments, what I care about or don't care about, what I see or don't see, what I am drawn to and what I am repelled by, what I can take for granted, where I can go, how others respond to me, and what I can ignore. Most of us would not choose to be socialized into racism and white supremacy. Unfortunately, we didn't have that choice. While there is variation in how these messages are conveyed and how much we internalize them, nothing could have exempted us from these messages completely. Now it is our responsibility to grapple with how this socialization manifests itself in our daily lives and how it shapes our responses when it is challenged.

CHAPTER 5

THE GOOD/BAD BINARY

He's not a racist. He is a really nice guy.

This chapter explores what is perhaps the most effective adaptation of racism in recent history: the good/bad binary.[1] Prior to the civil rights movement, it was socially acceptable for white people to openly proclaim their belief in their racial superiority. But when white Northerners saw the violence black people—including women and children—endured during the civil rights protests, they were appalled. These images became the archetypes of racists. After the civil rights movement, to be a good, moral person and to be complicit with racism became mutually exclusive. You could not be a good person and participate in racism; only bad people were racist. (These images of black persecution in the South during the civil rights movement of the 1960s also allowed Northern whites to position racists as always Southern.)

To accomplish this adaptation, racism first needed to be reduced to simple, isolated, and extreme acts of prejudice. These acts must be intentional, malicious, and based on conscious dislike of someone because of race. Racists were those white people in the South, smiling and picnicking at the base of lynching trees; store owners posting Whites Only signs over drinking fountains; and good ol' boys beating innocent children such as Emmett Till to death. In other words, racists were mean, ignorant, old, uneducated, Southern whites. Nice people, well-intended people, open-minded middle-class people, people raised in the "enlightened North," could not be racist.

RACIST = BAD	NOT RACIST = GOOD
Ignorant	Progressive
Bigoted	Educated
Prejudiced	Open-minded
Mean-spirited	Well-intentioned
Old	Young
Southern	Northern

While making racism bad seems like a positive change, we have to look at how this functions in practice. Within this paradigm, to suggest that I am racist is to deliver a deep moral blow—a kind of character assassination. Having received this blow, I must defend my character, and that is where all my energy will go—to deflecting the charge, rather than reflecting on my behavior. In this way, the good/bad binary makes it nearly impossible to talk to white people about racism, what it is, how it shapes all of us, and the inevitable ways that we are conditioned to participate in it. If we cannot discuss these dynamics or see ourselves within them, we cannot stop participating in racism. The good/bad binary made it effectively impossible for the average white person to understand—much less interrupt—racism.

As African American scholar and filmmaker Omowale Akintunde says: "Racism is a systemic, societal, institutional, omnipresent, and epistemologically embedded phenomenon that pervades every vestige of our reality. For most whites, however, racism is like murder: the concept exists, but someone has to commit it in order for it to happen. This limited view of such a multilayered syndrome cultivates the sinister nature of racism and, in fact, perpetuates racist phenomena rather than eradicates them."[2]

The good/bad frame is a false dichotomy. All people hold prejudices, especially across racial lines in a society deeply divided by race. I can be told that everyone is equal by my parents, I can have friends of color, and I may not tell racist jokes. Yet I am still affected by the forces of racism as a member of a society in which racism is the bedrock. I will still be seen as white, treated as white, and experience life as a white person. My identity, personality, interests, and investments will develop from a white perspective. I will have a white worldview and a white frame of reference. In a society in which race clearly matters, our race profoundly shapes us. If we want to challenge this construct, we must make an honest accounting of how it is manifest in our own lives and in the society around us.

Although individual racist acts do occur, these acts are part of a larger system of interlocking dynamics. The focus on individual incidences masks the personal, interpersonal, cultural, historical, and structural analysis that is necessary to challenge this larger system. The simplistic idea that racism is limited to individual intentional acts committed by unkind people is at the root of virtually all white defensiveness on this topic. To move beyond defensiveness, we have to let go of this common belief.

The good/bad binary certainly obscures the structural nature of racism and makes it difficult for us to see or understand. Equally problematic is the impact of such a worldview on our actions. If, as a white person, I conceptualize racism as a binary and I place myself on the "not racist" side, what further action is required of me? No action is required, because I am not a racist. Therefore, racism is not my problem; it doesn't concern me and there is nothing further I need to do. This worldview guarantees that I will not build my skills in thinking critically about racism or use my position to challenge racial inequality.

The good/bad binary is at play virtually every day in my work as a consultant on issues of racial justice. My job is to help individuals and organizations see how racism is manifesting itself in their practices and outcomes. I am typically received well when speaking in general terms—for example, "Your requirement that applicants have an advanced degree rather than equivalent experience is automatically disqualifying some of the applicants that could bring the perspectives and experiences you say you are looking for." Yet when I point out a concrete moment in the room in which someone's racism is manifesting itself, white fragility erupts.

For example, I was working with a group of educators who had been meeting regularly for at least eight sessions. The group was composed of the equity teams for a public school system, self-selected by people who wanted to support equity efforts in their schools. I had just finished an hour-long presentation titled "Seeing the Water: Whiteness in Daily Life." This presentation is designed to make visible the relentless messages of white superiority and the resulting and inevitable internalization of these messages for white people. The room appeared to be with me—open and receptive, with many nodding along in agreement. Then a white teacher raised her hand and told a story about an interaction she had as she drove alongside a group of parents protesting the achievement gap in her school. She then proceeded to imitate one mother in particular who offended her. "You don't understand our children!" this mother had called out to her as she drove by. By the stereotypical way that the white teacher imitated the mother, we all knew that the mother was black. The room seemed to collectively hold its breath at her imitation, which was bordering on racial mockery. While the teacher's concluding point was that, on reflection, she came to realize that the mother was right and that she really didn't understand children of color, the emotional thrust of the story was her umbrage at the mother for making this assumption. For the room, the emotional impact was on her stereotypical imitation of an angry black woman.

As this story came to a close, I had a decision to make. Should I act with integrity and point out what was racially problematic about the story? After all, making racism visible was literally what I had been hired to do. Further, several African American teachers in the room had certainly noticed the reinforcement of a racist stereotype. To not intervene would be, yet again, another white person choosing to protect white feelings rather than interrupt racism—a white person who billed herself as a racial justice consultant, no less! Yet I would be taking the risk of losing the group, given the likelihood that the woman would become defensive and shut down and the room would split into those who thought I had mistreated her and those who didn't. I decided to do what would retain my moral and professional integrity and serve as a model for other white people.

As diplomatically as possible, I said, "I understand that you gained valuable insight from that interaction and I thank you for sharing that insight with us. And I am going to ask you to consider not telling that story in that way again."

When she immediately began to protest, I interrupted her to continue. "I am offering you a teachable moment," I said, "and I am only asking that you to try to listen with openness." I then laid out what was racially problematic about how she told the story and offered her a way to share her learning without reinforcing racist stereotypes, for the same story could easily be told and the same conclusions drawn without the racially charged imitation of the mother.

She defensively interrupted me several times but eventually appeared to be listening. Shortly after this intervention, we took a break. Several African American teachers came up to thank me, as did one white teacher who found my intervention a refreshing and much-needed example of how to break with white solidarity. Several white people also approached to let me know how upset the teacher was and that she was quitting the group.

Thus is the power of the good/bad binary and how it informs white fragility. Even a white person on an equity team participating in a class based on the premise that racism is structured into our society and that white complicity is an inevitable result could not handle feedback on how her racism was unintentionally manifesting itself.

If you are white and have ever been challenged to look at your own racism—perhaps you told a problematic joke or made a prejudiced assumption and someone brought it to your attention—it is common to feel defensive. If you believe that you are being told you are a bad person, all your energy is likely to go toward denying this possibility and invalidating the messenger rather than trying to understand why what you've said or done is hurtful. You will probably respond with white fragility. But unfortunately, white fragility can only protect the problematic behavior you feel so defensive about; it does not demonstrate that you are an open person who has no problematic racial behavior.

The dominant paradigm of racism as discrete, individual, intentional, and malicious acts makes it unlikely that whites will acknowledge any of our actions as racism. For example, I often read about a government official, a teacher, or another public servant expressing shockingly racist statements and still insisting that he or she is not racist. Readers may recall a West Virginia county employee—Pamela Ramsey Taylor—who held a high-level position as director of county development and was suspended after posting racist remarks about First Lady Michelle Obama on Facebook ("It will be so refreshing to have a classy, beautiful, dignified First Lady back in the White House. I'm tired of seeing a [sic] Ape in heels"). The mayor of the city responded, "Just made my day Pam." Taylor's response to the ensuing uproar was, "My comment was not intended to be racist at all. I was referring to my day being made for change in the White House! I am truly sorry for any hard feeling this may have caused! Those who know me know that I'm not in any way racist!" Although Taylor was suspended (but eventually got her job back), I am left wondering what actually qualifies as racism in the white mind.

When I talk to white people about racism, I hear the same claims—rooted in the good/bad binary—made again and again. I organize these claims into two overall categories, both of which label the person as good and therefore not racist. The first set claims color blindness: "I don't see color [and/or race has no meaning to me]; therefore, I am free of racism." The second set claims to value diversity: "I know people of color [and/or have been near people of color, and/or have general fond regard for people of color]; therefore, I am free of racism." Both categories fundamentally rest on the good/bad binary. Although I organize these narratives into two overall categories, they can be and often are used interchangeably. They don't need to make sense; they

just need to position the speaker as a good person—free of racism—
and end the discussion.

Color-blind statements insist that people do not see race, or if
they see it, it has no meaning to them. Color-blind claims include the
following:

- I was taught to treat everyone the same.
- I don't see color.
- I don't care if you are pink, purple, or polka-dotted.
- Race doesn't have any meaning to me.
- My parents were/weren't racist, so that is why I am not racist.
- Everyone struggles, but if you work hard . . .
- So-and-so just happens to be black, but that has nothing to do
  with what I am about to tell you.
- Focusing on race is what divides us.
- If people are respectful to me, I am respectful to them, regardless
  of race.
- Children today are so much more open.
- I'm not racist; I'm from Canada.
- I was picked on because I was white/I grew up poor (so I don't
  have race privilege).

The second set I term *color-celebrate*. This set claims that the person sees and embraces racial difference. Color-celebrate claims include
statements such as these:

- I work in a very diverse environment.
- I have people of color in my family/married a person
  of color/have children of color.
- I was in the military.
- I used to live in New York/Hawaii.
- We don't like how white our neighborhood is, but we had
  to move here for the schools.

- I was in the Peace Corps.
- I marched in the sixties.
- We adopted a child from China.
- Our grandchildren are multiracial.
- I was on a mission in Africa.
- I went to a very diverse school/lived in a very diverse neighborhood.
- I lived in Japan and was a minority, so I know what it is like to be a minority.
- I lived among the [*fill-in-the-blank*] people, so I am actually a person of color.
- My great-grandmother was a Native American princess.

In my work to unravel the dynamics of racism, I have found a question that never fails me. This question is *not* "Is this claim true, or is it false?"; we will never come to an agreement on a question that sets up an either/or dichotomy on something as sensitive as racism. Instead I ask, "How does this claim function in the conversation?" If we apply this question to these two sets of narratives, one color-blind and the other color-celebrate, we see that all of these claims ultimately function in a similar way; they all exempt the person from any responsibility for or participation in the problem. They take race off the table, and they close (rather than open) any further exploration. In so doing, they protect the racial status quo.

These typical white racial claims depend on an underlying framework of meaning. Identifying this framework can help us understand how we manage to make such claims in the context of extreme segregation and racial inequity.

Imagine a pier stretching out over the water. Viewed from above, the pier appears to simply float there. The top of the pier—the part that we can see—signifies the surface aspect of these claims. Yet while the pier seems to float effortlessly, it is, of course, not floating at all; it is propped up by a structure submerged under the water. The pier rests on pillars embedded in the ocean floor. In the same way that a pier sits on submerged pillars that are not immediately visible, the beliefs supporting our racial claims are hidden from our view. To topple the pier, we need to access and uproot the pillars.

The above claims are all meant to provide evidence of the speaker's lack of racism. For example, in a conversation about racism, when white people say that they work in a diverse environment or that they have people of color in their family, they are giving me their evidence that they are not racist. If this is their evidence, how are they defining racism? In other words, what underlying system of meaning leads them to make that claim? If working near people of color is the evidence that distinguishes them from a racist, then evidently a racist cannot work near people of color. This claim rests on a definition of racism as *conscious intolerance*; a racist is someone who presumably cannot tolerate even the sight of a person of color. According to this logic, because they know or work with people of color, or lived in New York, where they saw people of color all around them, and have spoken with and smiled at people of color, they cannot participate in racism. When we go beneath the surface of these claims, we can see their superficiality, for even an avowed white nationalist who would march openly in the streets chanting "blood and soil!" can interact with people of color, and very likely does so. In fact, I have seen black reporters interviewing open and avowed white supremacists on television, with both parties proceeding calmly and respectfully.

Someone who claims to have been taught to treat everyone the same is simply telling me that he or she doesn't understand socialization. It is not possible to teach someone to treat everyone the same. We can be told, and often are told, to treat everyone the same, but we cannot successfully be taught to do so because human beings are not objective. Further, we wouldn't *want* to treat everyone the same because people have different needs and different relationships with us. Differential treatment in itself is not the problem. For example, I wouldn't give a document with a twelve-point font to a person with low vision, even though someone else wouldn't have any trouble reading it. The problem is the misinformation that circulates around us and causes our differential treatment to be inequitable.

The feedback I have heard repeatedly from people of color is that when they hear a white person claim to have been taught to treat everyone the same, they are not thinking, "All right! I am now talking to a woke white person!" Quite the opposite; some version of eye-rolling is taking place as they sign the white person off as unaware and brace themselves for yet another exchange based in white denial and invalidation.

As a culture, we don't claim that gender roles and gender conditioning disappear the moment we love someone of the "opposite" gender. I identify as a woman and am married to someone who identifies as a man, yet I would never say, "Because I am married to a man, I have a gender-free life." We understand that gender is a very deep social construct, that we have different experiences depending on our gender roles, assignments, and expressions, and that we will wrestle with these differences throughout the life of our relationship. Yet when the topic is race, we claim that it is completely inoperative if there is any level of fond regard. In an even more ludicrous form of reality, we even go as far as to claim that racial conditioning disappears if we can calmly walk by people of color on the streets of large cities.

While the implication that a racist could not tolerate knowing, working next to, or walking among people of color is rather ridiculous, the sad fact is many whites have no cross-racial friendships at all. Perhaps this is why we rely on such flimsy evidence to certify ourselves as racism-free. But even those that have cross-racial friendships and use these as evidence of their lack of racism still invoke the binary of racist = bad / not racist = good binary. They see their friendship as proof that they are on the not-racist side of the binary. Yet cross-racial friendships do not block out the dynamics of racism in the society at large, and these dynamics continue unabated. The white person will still receive white privilege that a friend of color does not, even when the two people engage in activities together. Nor do these friendships block out all the messages that we have internalized and that are reinforced in this society. In fact, racism invariably manifests itself within cross-racial friendships as well. Racism cannot be absent from your friendship. No person of color whom I've met has said that racism isn't at play in his or her friendships with white people. Some whites are more thoughtful, aware, and receptive to feedback than others, but no cross-racial relationship is free from the dynamics of racism in this society.

Many whites believe that if they are not talking about racism with their friends of color or if their friends are not giving them feedback about racism, then racism is a non-issue. But just because you and your friend don't talk about racism does not mean it isn't at play. Indeed, this silence is one of the ways that racism is manifest, for it is an imposed silence. Many people of color have told me that they initially tried to talk about racism with their white friends, but their friends got defensive or invalidated their experiences, so they stopped sharing their experiences. If racism is not a topic of discussion between a white person and a person of color who are friends, this absence of conversation may indicate a lack of cross-racial trust.

The good/bad binary is powerful and enduring. In what follows, I offer counternarratives to a few of its most popular claims. Notice how each of these claims labels the person making them as not racist, thereby exempting them from further involvement or responsibility.

"I was taught to treat everyone the same."

As explained above, no one can be taught to treat people equitably, because humans cannot be 100 percent objective. For example, I could lecture you for hours that it is not nice to judge, that no one likes to be judged—"You wouldn't want to be judged, would you?"—and so on. At the end of that lecture, you would still continue to judge, because it is impossible not to. We can try to examine our judgments, hold them more lightly, and so forth, but to be free of judgment? Not possible. Nor can we treat everyone the same. Indeed, the person professing to treat everyone the same is stating a value that he or she holds, but the claim closes off any further reflection. Once we understand the power of implicit bias, for example, we know that we must deepen rather than close off further reflection. Although deeper reflection won't free us of unconscious inequitable treatment of others, it will get us closer than will outright denial.

"I marched in the sixties."

Someone who tells me that they marched in the 1960s—like the person who tells me they know people of color—is telling me that they see racism as a simple matter of racial intolerance (which clearly they don't have or they could not have tolerated marching alongside black people during the civil rights movement). They are also telling me that they believe that racism is uncomplicated and unchanging. Yet in the 1960s, we thought race was biological. We used terms like *Oriental* and *colored*. Nevertheless, in the light of an action they took more than fifty years ago, they see their racial learning as finished for life. Their action certifies them as free of racism, and there is no more discussion or reflection required. It also assumes that absolutely no racism—even unconsciously—was perpetrated toward blacks by well-meaning whites during the civil rights movement. Yet the testimony of black civil rights activists tells us otherwise. How many white people who marched in the 1960s had authentic cross-racial relationships with African Americans?

Certainly there was (and still is) racial segregation throughout the North, too, perhaps not as explicitly enforced but surely enforced implicitly in countless ways. Perhaps many of those white Northerners who came down South to save black people had some patronizing or condescending attitudes? Might many have dominated discussions, not listened to others, and assumed to know what was best? Did they say many racially problematic things that Southern blacks were forced to endure? Had I been old enough, I probably would have marched in the 1960s, and yet as far as into the 1990s, I was saying and doing racially problematic things. Although I do them less often and less blatantly today, I still do them. Again, the claim that someone is not racist because the person marched in the 1960s rests on the simplistic definition of racism as a conscious intolerance of black people.

"I was the minority at my school,
so I was the one who experienced racism."

While everyone of every race holds prejudice and can discriminate against someone of another race, in the US and other white/settler nations, only white people are in the position to oppress people of color collectively and throughout the whole of society. This claim defines racism as a fluid dynamic that changes direction according to each group's ratio in a given space. While a white person may have been picked on—even mercilessly—by being in the numerical minority in a specific context, the individual was experiencing race prejudice and discrimination, *not racism*. This distinction is not meant to minimize the white person's experience, but aims to clarify and to prevent rendering the terms interchangeable and thus meaningless.

Moreover, the society at large is still reinforcing white supremacy, and everyone in the school was affected by it. It is likely that white students at such a school were treated better by teachers and that higher expectations were held for them. Their textbooks, the curriculum, and the administration still reinforced a preference for whiteness. Outside the school (and in many aspects within it), these students were still granted white privilege as they moved through society.

For most whites, being the minority in their school or neighborhood is usually temporary. They are probably no longer the minority in their environment as upward mobility generally entails moving away from integrated spaces or those in which people of color are the majority.

"My parents were not racist, and they taught me not to be racist."

Whether you define racism as racial prejudices and individual acts or as a system of racial inequality that benefits whites at the expense of people of color (as antiracists do), your parents could not have taught you not to be racist, and your parents could not have been free of racism themselves. A racism-free upbringing is not possible, because racism is a social system embedded in the culture and its institutions. We are born into this system and have no say in whether we will be affected by it. I understand that many parents tell their children to not be racist, but the practice of our lives is more powerful than the words we say, and living a segregated life is a powerful message of practice. Of course, there are degrees, and it is certainly more constructive to be told that racism is wrong rather than right, but that is still not enough to completely inoculate us from the culture at large.

Let's imagine that what the person really meant was this: "My parents were not racially prejudiced, and they taught me not to be racially prejudiced." This statement would still be false because it is not humanly possible to be free of prejudice. This statement simply indicates that the person is uneducated about the socialization process and the inescapable dynamics of human culture. A person's parents might have said that they were not prejudiced and thus denied their prejudice. They may have told their children that they should not be prejudiced, the result being that, like their parents, the children deny their prejudice. The parents may have sincerely hoped and believed that they were raising their children to not be prejudiced. But we can't teach humans to have no prejudice at all. The human brain just does not work that way as we process information about others. Most of us only teach our children not to admit to prejudice. A parent training a child not to say certain things that are overtly racist is teaching the child self-censorship rather than how to examine the deeply embedded racial messages we all absorb. Ideally, we would teach our children how to recognize and challenge prejudice, rather than deny it.

"Children today are so much more open."

As for the claim that children are so much more open, research over the past two decades indicates that children are vastly more sophisticated in their awareness of racial hierarchies than most people believe.[3] Even when race is not explicitly discussed, children internalize both implicit and explicit messages about it from their environment.

For example, psychology researchers Maria Monteiro, Dalila de França, and Ricardo Rodrigues tested 283 white children aged six to seven, and nine to ten years old. The children were asked to allocate money to white and black children, sometimes with a white adult in the room and sometimes with no adult in the room, to see if having an adult present influenced their behavior. The researchers found that the younger group discriminated against black children in both conditions, while the older group discriminated against the black children only when no adult was present. This finding is significant because it shows that the older children clearly had racial prejudice and acted on it, but hid it when a white adult was present. Thus, the children showed that they did not become less racially biased with age, but that they had learned to hide their racism in front of adults.[4] Monteiro and her colleagues found racial hostility in white children as young as three years old. However, most white parents and teachers believe that children are color-blind.[5] This false belief keeps us from honestly addressing racism with children and exploring with them how racism has shaped the inequities that they already observe.

"Race has nothing to do with it."

How often have we heard someone preface a story about race with the statement, "Race had nothing to do with this, but . . ." or "She just happened to be black, and . . ."? Let's look closer at why the person feels that it is necessary to make this opening point, as it usually illustrates just the opposite. The racist = bad / not racist = good binary is reflected in these statements because according to the binary, if race had anything to do with it, then the person telling the story would be racially implicated and thus no longer positioned as color-blind or outside race. Further, if the story is about a conflict between the storyteller and a person of color, then the storyteller might sound racist, and that would mean that the speaker is a bad person. If, however, the speaker understands racism as an institutional system into which we are all socialized, then he or she wouldn't make this disclaimer because the person understands that the conflict cannot be free of racial dimensions.

We bring our racial histories with us, and contrary to the ideology of individualism, we represent our groups and those who have come before us. Our identities are not unique or inherent but constructed or produced through social processes. What's more, we don't see through clear or objective eyes—we see through racial lenses. On some level, race is always at play, even in its supposed absence.

"Focusing on race is what divides us."

The idea that talking about racism is itself racist has always struck me as odd. It is rooted in the concept that race doesn't matter; thus, to talk about it gives it undeserved weight. Many things that we talk about every day don't really matter. Precisely because these topics of conversation don't matter, they are easy to talk about. We know race matters a great deal, but for many of the reasons already discussed, we feel the need to deny its importance. Ironically, this denial is a fundamental way in which white people maintain unequal racial power.

I have heard this response many times in the context of cross-racial discussions, most often at the point in which white racial power is named. Many whites see the naming of white racial power as divisive. For them, the problem is not the power inequity itself; the problem is *naming* the power inequity. This naming breaks the pretense of unity and exposes the reality of racial division.

Even though participants of color repeatedly state that whites' refusal to acknowledge racial difference and power dynamics actually maintains racial inequity, white participants continue to insist that not talking about difference is necessary for unity. Although the participants are purportedly engaged in these discussions to explore differences in racial perspectives and experiences, as soon as these differences appear, many whites react as if there has been a violation. Of course, white norms *are* violated by naming white power. But unequal power relations cannot be challenged if they are not acknowledged.

Refusing to engage in an authentic exploration of racial realities erases (and denies) alternate racial experiences. If we block out other realities by not discussing them, we can pretend that they don't exist, thereby assuming a shared racial experience. Not talking about race allows us to maintain our sense of ourselves as unique individuals, outside collective socialization and group experience. While it isn't comfortable for most whites to talk about racism, we must do so if we want to challenge—rather than protect—racism. To avoid talking about racism can only hold our misinformation in place and prevent us from developing the necessary skills and perspectives to challenge the status quo.

IN CONCLUSION

Most of us alive before and during the 1960s have had images from the civil rights conflicts of that time held up as the epitome of racism. Today we have images of white nationalists marching in Charlottesville, Virginia, to hold up. And while speaking up against these explicitly racist actions is critical, we must also be careful not to use them to keep ourselves on the "good" side of a false binary. I have found it much more useful to think of myself as on a continuum. Racism is so deeply woven into the fabric of our society that I do not see myself escaping from that continuum in my lifetime. But I can continually seek to move further along it. I am not in a fixed position on the continuum; my position is dictated by what I am actually doing at a given time. Conceptualizing myself on an active continuum changes the question from whether I am or am not racist to a much more constructive question: Am I actively seeking to interrupt racism in this context? And perhaps even more importantly, how do I know?

CHAPTER 6

ANTI-BLACKNESS

> *But all our phrasing—race relations, racial chasm,*
> *racial justice, racial profiling, white privilege, even white*
> *supremacy—serves to obscure that racism is a visceral*
> *experience, that it dislodges brains, blocks airways, rips*
> *muscle, extracts organs, cracks bones, breaks teeth. . . .*
> *You must always remember that the sociology, the history,*
> *the economics, the graphs, the charts, the regressions*
> *all land, with great violence, upon the body.*
>
> —Ta-Nehisi Coates, *Between the World and Me*

Racism is complex and nuanced, and its manifestations are not the same for every group of color. To challenge the ideologies of racism such as individualism and color blindness, we as white people must suspend our perception of ourselves as unique and/or outside race. Exploring our collective racial identity interrupts a key privilege of dominance—the ability to see oneself only as an individual. We need to discuss white people as a group—even if doing so jars us—in order to disrupt our unracialized identities.

For people of color, the privilege of being seen (and seeing themselves) as unique individuals outside the context of race cannot be taken for granted. Talking about race and racism in general terms such as *white people* is constructive for whites because it interrupts individualism. But racial generalization also reinforces something problematic for people of color—the continual focus on their group identity. Furthermore, it collapses many racial groups into one generic category, thereby denying the specific ways that different groups experience racism. While people of color share some experiences of racism overall, there are also variations based on a specific group's history. These variations include how group members have adapted to the dominant culture, how they have been represented, how they have been positioned in relation to other groups of color, and the "role" the group has been assigned by dominant society. The messages I have internalized about people of Asian heritage, for example, are not the same as those I have internalized for Indigenous people, and a key aspect of challenging these messages is to identify their differences and how they shape my attitudes toward various groups of color. Further, there are myriad groups within these categories, and I have different attitudes here too. For example, my stereotypes about Japanese people are not the same as my stereotypes about Chinese people, and these stereotypes inform different responses.

In this chapter, I will address the uniquely anti-black sentiment integral to white identity. In doing so, I do not wish to minimize the racism that other groups of color experience. However, I believe that in the white mind, black people are the ultimate racial "other," and we must grapple with this relationship, for it is a foundational aspect of the racial socialization underlying white fragility.

I remind my readers that I am addressing white people at the societal level. I have friends who are black and whom I love deeply. I do not have to suppress feelings of hatred and contempt as I sit with them; I see their humanity. But on the macro level, I also recognize the deep anti-black feelings that have been inculcated in me since childhood. These feelings surface immediately—in fact, before I can even think—when I conceptualize black people in general. The sentiments arise when I pass black strangers on the street, see stereotypical depictions of black people in the media, and hear the thinly veiled warnings and jokes passed between white people. These are the deeper feelings that I need to be willing to examine, for these feelings can and do seep out without my awareness and hurt those whom I love.

As discussed in previous chapters, we live in a culture that circulates relentless messages of white superiority. These messages exist simultaneously with relentless messages of black inferiority. But anti-blackness goes deeper than the negative stereotypes all of us have absorbed; anti-blackness is foundational to our very identities as white people. Whiteness has always been predicated on blackness. As discussed in chapter 2, there was no concept of race or a white race before the need to justify the enslavement of Africans. Creating a separate and inferior black race simultaneously created the "superior" white race: one concept could not exist without the other. In this sense, whites need black people; blackness is essential to the creation of white identity.

Scholars have argued that whites split off from themselves and project onto black people the aspects that we don't want to own in ourselves.[1] For example, the white masters of enslaved Africans consistently depicted the Africans as lazy and childlike, even as they toiled at back-breaking work from sunup to sundown. Today, we depict blacks as dangerous, a portrayal that perverts the true direction of violence between whites and blacks since the founding of this country. This characterization causes aversion and hostility toward black people and feelings of superiority toward ourselves, but we cannot morally acknowledge any of these feelings. To reiterate, I am speaking here of the collective white consciousness. An individual white person may not be explicitly aware of these feelings, but I am often amazed at how quickly they surface with even the slightest challenge.

Consider the enduring white resentment about the perceived injustices of affirmative action programs. There is empirical evidence that people of color (especially black people) have been discriminated against in hiring since the ending of enslavement and into the present.[2] In the late 1960s, a program was instituted to help ameliorate this discrimination: affirmative action.

There is a great amount of misinformation about affirmative action, as evidenced in the idea of special rights. For example, people commonly believe that if a person of color applies for a position, he or she must be hired over a white person; that black people are given preferential treatment in hiring; and that a specific number of people of color must be hired to fill a quota.

All these beliefs are patently untrue. Affirmative action is a tool to ensure that *qualified* minority applicants are given the same employment opportunities as white people. It is a flexible program—there are no quotas or requirements as commonly understood. Moreover, *white women* have been the greatest beneficiaries of affirmative action, although the program did not initially include them. Corporations are more likely to favor white women and immigrants of color of elite backgrounds from outside the United States when choosing their executives.[3] No employer is required to hire an unqualified person of color, but companies are required to be able to articulate why they didn't hire a qualified person of color (and this requirement is rarely enforced). Additionally, affirmative action never applied to private companies—only to state and governmental agencies.

Still, this program has been systematically chipped away at, and several states have eliminated affirmative action programs altogether. In turn, African Americans continue to be the most underrepresented group at the organizational leadership level. In 2018, affirmative action has all but been dismantled. Yet invariably, I will encounter a white male—bristling with umbrage—who raises the issue of affirmative action. It seems that we white people just cannot let go of our outrage over how unfair this toothless attempt to rectify centuries of injustice has been to *us*. And this umbrage consistently surfaces in overwhelmingly white leadership groups that have asked me to come in and help them recruit and retain more people of color.

Copious research attests to the disdain of whites for African Americans, from the school-to-prison pipeline, to mass incarceration, to white flight.[4] For example, on attitude surveys, most whites say they would prefer neighborhoods that are no more than 30 percent black, and more than half of whites say they would not move into a neighborhood that is 30 percent black or more. Studies of actual mobility patterns not only confirm these preferences, but also show that whites downplay them. White flight has been triggered when a formerly white neighborhood reaches 7 percent black, and in neighborhoods with more than a few black families, white housing demand tends to disappear.[5] (That is, the demand disappears unless white people need that housing because of unaffordable home prices in other neighborhoods. In that case, black people are pushed out as gentrification increases. Brooklyn, Harlem, Oakland, and Seattle are prime examples.)

A 2015 study by the American Sociological Foundation found that the highest level of segregation is between blacks and whites, the lowest is between Asians and whites, and the level between Latinx and whites occupies an intermediate position. A majority of whites, in both the expression of their beliefs and the practice of their lives, do not want to integrate with blacks.

We see anti-black sentiment in how quickly images of brutality toward black children (let alone black adults) are justified by the white assumption that it must have been deserved. Such beliefs would be unimaginable if we had been shown images of white teens being thrown across schoolrooms, of white kindergarteners handcuffed, of a white child shot while playing with a toy gun in the park. We see anti-black sentiment in the immediate rejoinder to Black Lives Matter that *all* lives matter, that *blue* lives matter. And in the absurdly false comparison between the white nationalist and "alt-right" movement (now directly connected to the White House) with the Black Panther Party of the 1960s. We see anti-blackness in how much more harshly we criticize blacks, by every measure. We see it in the president of the United States positioning the avowed white supremacist neo-Nazis marching openly in the streets—including one man who drove a car into a crowd of protesters—as equal in character to the people protesting them. As Coates notes in "The Case for Reparations":

> The early American economy was built on slave labor. The Capitol and the White House were built by slaves. President James K. Polk traded slaves from the Oval Office. The laments about "black pathology," the criticism of black family structures by pundits and intellectuals, ring hollow in a country whose existence was predicated on the torture of

black fathers, on the rape of black mothers, on the sale of black children. An honest assessment of America's relationship to the black family reveals the country to be not its nurturer but its destroyer. And this destruction did not end with slavery.[6]

Anti-blackness is rooted in misinformation, fables, perversions, projections, and lies. It is also rooted in a lack of historical knowledge and an inability or unwillingness to trace the effects of history into the present. But perhaps most fundamentally, anti-blackness comes from deep guilt about what we have done and continue to do; the unbearable knowledge of our complicity with the profound torture of black people from past to present. While the full trauma of this torture in its various forms—both physically and psychologically—is only borne by African Americans, there is a kind of moral trauma in it for the white collective. In his revolutionary book, *My Grandmother's Hands*, social worker and therapist Resmaa Menakem refers to white supremacy as *white body supremacy* to argue that white supremacy is a form of trauma that is stored in our collective bodies: "Many African Americans know trauma intimately—from their own nervous systems, from the experiences of people they love, and, most often, from both. But African Americans are not alone in this. A different but equally real form of racialized trauma lives in the bodies of most white Americans."[7] Our projections allow us to bury this trauma by dehumanizing and then blaming the victim. If blacks are not human in the same ways that we white people are human, our mistreatment of them doesn't count. We are not guilty; they are. If they are bad, it isn't unfair. In fact, it is *righteous*.

There is a curious satisfaction in the punishment of black people: the smiling faces of the white crowd picnicking at lynchings in the past, and the satisfied approval of white people observing mass incarceration and execution in the present. White righteousness, when inflicting pain on African Americans, is evident in the glee the white collective derives from blackface and depictions of blacks as apes and gorillas. We see it in the compassion toward white people who are addicted to opiates and the call to provide them with services versus the mandatory sentencing perpetrated against those addicted to crack. We see it in the concern about the "forgotten" white working class so critical to the outcome of the last presidential election, with no concern for blacks, who remain on the bottom of virtually every social and economic measure. As Coates points out, "toiling blacks are in their proper state; toiling whites raise the specter of white slavery."[8]

Coates refers to white people as "Dreamers" in "the Dream," falsely believing that they are actually white. I take this to mean that whites can only be white if someone is not white—if someone is the opposite of white. White is a false identity, an identity of false superiority. In that sense, whiteness isn't real. The dream is the "perfect world," unpolluted by blacks. If whites are to construct this world, blacks must be separated through state violence. Yet they still must exist, for the existence of blacks provides the needed other against which whites may rise. Thus, white identity depends in particular on the projection of inferiority onto blacks and the oppression this inferior status justifies for the white collective.

To put it bluntly, I believe that the white collective fundamentally hates blackness for what it reminds us of: that we are capable and guilty of perpetrating immeasurable harm and that our gains come through the subjugation of others. We have a particular hatred for "uppity" blacks, those who dare to step out of their place and look us in the eye as equals.[9] The messages that circulate relentlessly across the generations reinforce the white belief that blacks are inherently undeserving (a frankly outrageous belief, given the state-sanctioned robbery of their labor). We heard this message in the narrative of "welfare cheats" and "welfare queens" in the Reagan era. We see it today when commentators slam National Football League (NFL) players who kneel during the national anthem and exercise their right to protest police brutality as "ungrateful" and when former congressman Joe Walsh declares that Stevie Wonder is "another ungrateful black multimillionaire." We see it when Robert Jeffress, Dallas evangelical pastor and adviser to the president of the United States, claims that NFL players who protest police brutality against African Americans should thank God they don't have to worry about being shot in the head "like they would be in North

Korea." We see it in the outrage of the crowd of white progressives who showed up to hear Bernie Sanders speak in Seattle and were asked by black activists to grant four and a half minutes of silence to honor Michael Brown, an unarmed black man shot by police in Ferguson, Missouri: "How dare you!" the crowd cried.

Carol Anderson, in her book *White Rage*, argues that "the trigger for white rage, inevitably, is black advancement. It is not the mere presence of black people that is the problem; rather, it is blackness with ambition, with drive, with purpose, with aspirations, and with demands for full and equal citizenship. It is blackness that refuses to accept subjugation, to give up." She continues: "The truth is that, despite all this, a black man was elected president of the United States: the ultimate advancement, and thus the ultimate affront. Perhaps not surprisingly, voting rights were severely curtailed, the federal government was shut down, and more than once the Office of the President was shockingly, openly, and publicly disrespected by other elected officials."[10]

Anti-blackness is a complex and confusing stew of resentment and benevolence, for we also use blacks to feel warmhearted and noble. We are drawn to those who cast their eyes downward in our presence, the ones we can "save" from the horrors of their black lives with our abundance and kindness. Consider an example I often use in my presentations: *The Blind Side*, a hugely popular movie for which Sandra Bullock received an Academy Award. This film is a cogent example of whites as the racially benevolent side of the coin. The film is based on the "true" story of a family—the Tuohys—who rescued Michael Oher, a black man who came from impoverished family circumstances and who went on to become an NFL player. Although the movie was popular with white audiences, many problematic racial narratives are reinscribed in the film. In fact, there are no black characters who do *not* reinforce negative racial stereotypes. Oher himself is portrayed as a childlike gentle giant who lives in abject poverty. Sprinkled in are his drug-addicted single mother with multiple children from unknown fathers, the incompetent welfare worker, the uppity lawyer, and the menacing gang members in his drug-infested and crime-ridden neighborhood.

In one pivotal scene, Oher returns to his former neighborhood. As he walks down the street, he is surrounded by a gang that tries to intimidate him. While he considers his limited options, Mrs. Tuohy arrives and confronts the gang members, who quickly back down and retreat. Rescued by Mrs. Tuohy, Oher is returned back to safe white suburbia. The scene makes it clear: the only way Oher could be saved from the terrors of his own black community is through the benevolence and bravery of a white family.

In the film, white professionals discuss Oher as if he were developmentally disabled (he certainly comes off as such—he is passive and inarticulate throughout the movie). His teachers note that on his IQ test, he scored in the bottom percentile in "ability to learn" but in the top percentile in "protective instinct"! As a professor of education who has never heard of a test measuring "protective instinct," I have been unable to find evidence of this bizarre measurement. It is highly problematic that Oher, as a black male, is portrayed as severely lacking in intellectual abilities but exceptional in something instinctual. His limited intellectual capacity is reinforced throughout the film, for example, when the youngest child of the Tuohy household has to teach Oher how to play football.

According to the film, Oher is never able to understand the rules of the game, so Mrs. Tuohy appeals to his "protective instinct" by telling him to pretend one of his new white family members is going to be hurt. Once his instincts are engaged (rather than his intellect), he is unstoppable on the field. In a particularly insulting scene, the white child who tried unsuccessfully to teach Oher how to play football sits at a table negotiating a contract for him with powerful adult men while Oher sits in the background, mute.

This film, told from the white perspective and enthusiastically received by audiences, reinforces some very important dominant ideologies:

- White people are the saviors of black people.
- Some black children may be innocent, but black adults are morally and criminally corrupt.

- Whites who are willing to save or otherwise help black people, at seemingly great personal cost, are noble, courageous, and morally superior to other whites.
- Individual black people can overcome their circumstances, but usually only with the help of white people.
- Black neighborhoods are inherently dangerous and criminal.
- Virtually all blacks are poor, incompetent, and unqualified for their jobs; they belong to gangs, are addicted to drugs, and are bad parents.
- The most dependable route for black males to escape the "inner city" is through sports.
- White people are willing to deal with individual "deserving" black people, but whites do not become a part of the black community in any meaningful way (beyond charity work).[11]

Of course, Oher also brings redemption to the whites who save him. The film ends with a voice-over from Mrs. Tuohy, a Christian, claiming it was God's will that this boy be saved (presumably because his talent on the field made him more profitable and thus valuable to white people). The Tuohys, of course, are the good whites, who have to deal with the prejudice of the individual bad whites they encounter at the country club and other places. In this way, the racist = bad / not racist = good binary is also reinforced. The film is fundamentally and insidiously anti-black.

White racial socialization engenders many conflicting feelings toward African Americans: benevolence, resentment, superiority, hatred, and guilt roil barely below the surface and erupt at the slightest breach, yet can never be explicitly acknowledged. Our need to deny the bewildering manifestations of anti-blackness that reside so close to the surface makes us irrational, and that irrationality is at the heart of white fragility and the pain it causes people of color.

CHAPTER 7

RACIAL TRIGGERS
FOR WHITE PEOPLE

In a cross-racial dialogue at an organization that is trying to increase its staff's racial understanding, the participants of color repeatedly challenge the problematic assumptions in a white woman's statements. "I feel like everything I say is thrown back at me!" she exclaims. "White people are being attacked and blamed, and we have to defend ourselves or just be used as punching bags. I give up! I am not saying anything else."

The only black woman on a workplace planning team listens attentively to her white colleagues for the first hour of a meeting and then asks a question about their proposal. After the meeting, her supervisor calls her into her office and informs her that the other women felt attacked by her.

The factors discussed in the previous chapters insulate white people from race-based stress. Although white racial insulation is somewhat mediated by social class (with poor and working-class urban whites being generally less racially insulated than suburban or rural whites), the larger social environment protects whites as a group through institutions, cultural representations, media, school textbooks, movies, advertising, dominant discourses, and the like. Whiteness studies scholar Michelle Fine describes this insulation: "Whiteness accrues privilege and status; gets itself surrounded by protective pillows of resources and/or benefits of the doubt; how Whiteness repels gossip and voyeurism and instead demands dignity."[1] White people seldom find themselves without this protection. Or if they do, it is because they have chosen to temporarily step outside this area of safety. But within their insulated environment of racial privilege, whites both expect racial comfort and become less tolerant of racial stress.

When ideologies such as color blindness, meritocracy, and individualism are challenged, intense emotional reactions are common. I have discussed several reasons why whites are so defensive about the suggestion that we benefit from, and are complicit in, a racist system:

- Social taboos against talking openly about race
- The racist = bad / not racist = good binary
- Fear and resentment toward people of color
- Our delusion that we are objective individuals
- Our guilty knowledge that there is more going on than we can or will admit to
- Deep investment in a system that benefits us and that we have been conditioned to see as fair
- Internalized superiority and sense of a right to rule
- A deep cultural legacy of anti-black sentiment

Most white people have limited information about what racism is and how it works. For many white people, an isolated course taken in college or required "cultural competency training" in their workplace is the only time they may encounter a direct and sustained challenge to their racial reality. But even in this arena, not all multicultural courses or training programs talk directly about racism, much less address white privilege. It is far more the norm for these courses and programs to use racially coded language such as "urban," "inner city," and "disadvantaged," but rarely use "white" or "over-advantaged" or "privileged."

This racially coded language reproduces racist images and perspectives while simultaneously reproducing the comfortable illusion that race and its problems are what "they" have, not us. Reasons that the facilitators of these courses and trainings may not directly name the dynamics and beneficiaries of racism range from the lack of a valid analysis of racism by white facilitators, personal and economic survival strategies for facilitators of color, and pressure from management to keep the content comfortable and palatable for whites.

However, if and when an educational program does directly address racism and the privileging of whites, common white responses include anger, withdrawal, emotional incapacitation, guilt, argumentation, and cognitive dissonance (all of which reinforce the pressure on facilitators to avoid directly addressing racism). So-called progressive whites may not respond with anger but still insulate themselves via claims that they are beyond the need for engaging with the content because they "already had a class on this" or "already know this." All these responses constitute white fragility—the result of the reduced psychosocial stamina that racial insulation inculcates.

I was a full adult, a parent, and a college graduate before I ever experienced a challenge to my racial identity or position, and that experience was only because I had taken a position as a diversity trainer. When you combine this rarity with my lifetime of racial centrality, internalized superiority, sense of myself as a unique individual, and expectation for racial comfort that our culture engenders, I simply never had been called upon to build my capacity to endure racial stress.

Anthropologist Pierre Bourdieu's concept of *habitus* is very useful for understanding white fragility—the predictability of the white response to having our racial positions challenged.[2] According to Bourdieu, habitus is the result of socialization, the repetitive practices of actors and their interactions with each other and with the rest of their social environment. Because it is repetitive, our socialization produces and reproduces thoughts, perceptions, expressions, and actions. Thus, habitus can be thought of as a person's familiar ways of perceiving, interpreting, and responding to the social cues around him or her.

There are three key aspects of Bourdieu's theory that are relevant to white fragility: field, habitus, and capital. *Field* is the specific social context the person is in—a party, the workplace, or a school. If we take a school as an example, there is the macro field of school as a whole, and within the school are micro fields—the teacher's lounge, the staff room, the classroom, the playground, the principal's office, the nurses' office, the janitor's supply room, and so on.

Capital is the social value people hold in a particular field; how they perceive themselves and are perceived by others in terms of their power or status. For example, compare the capital of a teacher and a student, a teacher and a principal, a middle-class student and a student on free or reduced lunch, an English language learner and a native English speaker, a popular girl and an unpopular one, a custodian and a receptionist, a kindergarten teacher and a sixth-grade teacher, and so on.

Capital can shift with the field, for example, when the custodian comes "upstairs" to speak to the receptionist—the custodian in work clothes and the receptionist in business attire—the office worker has more capital than does the maintenance person. But when the receptionist goes "down" to the supply room, which the custodian controls, to request more whiteboard markers, those power lines shift; this is the domain of the custodian, who can fulfill the request quickly or can make the transaction difficult. Notice how race, class, and gender will also be at play in negotiations of power. The custodian is most likely to be male, and the receptionist female; the custodian more likely a person of color and the receptionist more likely white. These complex and intersecting layers of capital are being negotiated automatically.

Habitus includes a person's internalized awareness of his or her status, as well as responses to the status of others. In every field, people are (often unconsciously) vying for power, and each field will have rules of the game.[3] Habitus will depend on the power position the person occupies in the social structure. Returning to the school example, there will be different rules to gain power at the reception desk versus the custodian's supply room. These rules do not have to be thought about consciously—I automatically shift into them as I enter each field. If I don't follow these rules, I will be pushed out of that field through various means. Some of these rules are explicitly taught to us, while others are unwritten and learned by picking up consistent social patterns. For example, the rules spell out what we do or don't talk about in a given field and how to respond when someone talks about something considered taboo in that field.

When there is disequilibrium in the habitus—when social cues are unfamiliar and/or when they challenge our capital—we use strategies to regain our balance. Habitus maintains our social comfort and helps us regain it when those around us do not act in familiar and acceptable ways. We don't respond consciously to disequilibrium in the habitus; we respond unconsciously. Bourdieu explains that "habitus is neither a result of free will, nor determined by structures, but created by a kind of interplay between the two over time: dispositions that are both shaped by past events and structures, and that shape current practices and structures and also, importantly, that condition our very perceptions of these."[4] In this sense, habitus is created and reproduced "without any deliberate pursuit of coherence . . . without any conscious concentration."[5] In the rare situation in which the white position is challenged, disequilibrium results.

Thus, white fragility is a state in which even a minimum amount of racial stress in the habitus becomes intolerable, triggering a range of defensive moves. These moves include the outward display of emotions such as anger, fear, and guilt and behaviors such as argumentation, silence, and leaving the stress-inducing situation. These behaviors, in turn, reinstate white racial equilibrium. Racial stress results from an interruption to the racially familiar. These interruptions can take a variety of forms and come from a range of sources, including

- Suggesting that a white person's viewpoint comes from a racialized frame of reference (challenge to objectivity)
- People of color talking directly about their own racial perspectives (challenge to white taboos on talking openly about race)

- People of color choosing not to protect white people's feelings about race (challenge to white racial expectations and the need for, or entitlement to, racial comfort)
- People of color being unwilling to tell their stories or answer questions about their racial experiences (challenge to the expectation that people of color will serve us)
- A fellow white disagreeing with our racial beliefs (challenge to white solidarity)
- Receiving feedback that our behavior had a racist impact (challenge to white racial innocence)
- Suggesting that group membership is significant (challenge to individualism)
- An acknowledgment that access is unequal between racial groups (challenge to meritocracy)
- Being presented with a person of color in a position of leadership (challenge to white authority)
- Being presented with information about other racial groups through, for example, movies in which people of color drive the action but are not in stereotypical roles, or multicultural education (challenge to white centrality)
- Suggesting that white people do not represent or speak for all of humanity (challenge to universalism)

In a society in which whites are dominant, each of these challenges becomes exceptional. In turn, we are often at a loss for how to respond constructively. For example, I was once asked to provide one-on-one mentoring for a white male teacher who had made inappropriate racial comments to a black female student. When the girl's mother complained, the teacher became defensive and the conflict escalated. The incident ended up in the newspaper, and potential legal action was discussed. I will call this teacher Mr. Roberts. During one of our sessions, Mr. Roberts told me about his colleague, a white female teacher, who recently had two black students at her desk. She prefaced something she said to one of them with "Girl." The student was clearly taken aback and asked, "Did you just call me girl?" The other student said it was OK; the teacher called all her students girl.

In relaying this story to me, Mr. Roberts expressed his and his colleague's anger about having to be "so careful" and not being able to "say anything anymore." They perceived my intervention as a form of punishment and believed that because of the incident with him, students of color were now "oversensitive" and complaining about racism where it did not exist. For these teachers, the student's reaction to being called "Girl" was an example of this oversensitivity. This accusation is a familiar white narrative, and in this instance, it was rationalized for two reasons: First, because the teacher called all her female students "Girl," the comment had nothing to do with race. Second, one of the students didn't have an issue with the comment, so the student who did was seen as overreacting.

These white teachers' responses illustrate several dynamics of white fragility. First, the teachers never considered that in not understanding the student's reaction, they might be lacking some knowledge or context. They demonstrated no curiosity about the student's perspective or why she might have taken offense. Nor did they show concern about the student's feelings. They were unable to separate intentions from impact. Despite Mr. Roberts's lack of cross-racial skills and understanding—a lack that led to a racial violation with potential legal repercussions—he arrogantly remained confident that he was right and that the student was wrong. His colleague, aware that Mr. Roberts was in serious trouble about a cross-racial incident, still maintained white solidarity with him by validating their shared perspective and invalidating that of the student of color. The teachers used the student witness who excused the comment as proof that the other student was wrong. According to them, the witness was the correct student because she denied any racial implications. Finally, the teachers used this interaction as an opportunity to increase racial divides rather than bridge them and to protect their worldviews and positions.

White fragility may be conceptualized as a response or "condition" produced and reproduced by the continual social and material advantages of whiteness. When disequilibrium occurs—when there is an interruption to that which is familiar and taken for granted—white fragility restores equilibrium and returns the capital "lost" via the challenge. This capital includes self-image, control, and white solidarity. Anger toward the trigger, shutting down and/or tuning out, indulgence in emotional incapacitation such as guilt or "hurt feelings," exiting, or a combination of these responses results. Again, these strategies are reflexive and seldom conscious, but that does not make them benign.

CHAPTER 8

THE RESULT: WHITE FRAGILITY

I am coaching a small group of white employees on how racism manifests in their workplace. One member of the group, Karen, is upset about a request from Joan, her only colleague of color, to stop talking over her. Karen doesn't understand what talking over Joan has to do with race; she is an extrovert and tends to talks over everyone. I try to explain how the impact is different when we interrupt across race because we bring our histories with us. While Karen sees herself as a unique individual, Joan sees Karen as a white individual. Being interrupted and talked over by white people is not a unique experience for Joan; nor is it separate from the larger cultural context. Karen exclaims, "Forget it! I can't say anything right, so I am going to stop talking!"

The preceding episode highlights Karen's white fragility. She is unable to see herself in racial terms. When she is pressed to do so, she refuses to engage further, positioning herself as the one being treated unfairly. As NPR's Don Gonyea points out, a remarkable preponderance of white Americans believe that they also experience racial prejudice:

A majority of whites say discrimination against them exists in America today, according to a poll released Tuesday from NPR, the Robert Wood Johnson Foundation and the Harvard T. H. Chan School of Public Health.

"If you apply for a job, they seem to give the blacks the first crack at it," said 68-year-old Tim Hershman of Akron, Ohio, "and, basically, you know, if you want any help from the government, if you're white, you don't get it. If you're black, you get it."

More than half of whites—55 percent—surveyed say that, generally speaking, they believe there is discrimination against white people in America today. . . .

Notable, however, is that though a majority of whites in the poll say discrimination against them exists, a much smaller percentage say they have actually experienced it.[1]

The large body of research about children and race demonstrates that children start to construct their ideas about race very early. Remarkably, a sense of white superiority and knowledge of racial power codes appear to develop as early as preschool.[2] Professor of communications Debian Marty describes white children's upbringing:

As in other Western nations, white children born in the United States inherit the moral predicament of living in a white supremacist society. Raised to experience their racially based advantages as fair and normal, white children receive little if any instruction regarding the predicament they face, let alone any guidance in how to resolve it. Therefore, they experience or learn about racial tension without understanding Euro-Americans' historical responsibility for it and knowing virtually nothing about their contemporary roles in perpetuating it.[3]

Despite its ubiquity, white superiority is also unnamed and denied by most whites. If we become adults who explicitly oppose racism, as do many, we often organize our identity around a denial of our racially based privileges that reinforce racist disadvantage for others. What is particularly problematic about this contradiction is that white people's moral objection to racism increases their resistance to acknowledging their complicity with it. In a white supremacist context, white identity largely rests on a foundation of (superficial) racial tolerance and acceptance. We whites who position ourselves as liberal often opt to protect what we perceive as our moral reputations, rather than recognize or change our participation in systems of inequity and domination.

For example, in 2016, the Oscars were challenged for their lack of diversity. When asked if she felt the Oscars were "behind the times" for failing to nominate a single black actor for the second year in a row, actor Helen Mirren defaulted to white racial innocence in her reply: "It just so happened it went that way." She also claimed, "It's unfair to attack the academy." Actor Charlotte Rampling called the idea of a boycott against the Oscars to draw attention to the lack of diversity "racist against whites." In so responding, whites invoke the power to choose when, how, and to what extent racism is addressed or challenged. Thus, pointing out white advantage will often trigger patterns of confusion, defensiveness, and righteous indignation. These responses enable defenders to protect their moral character against a perceived attack while rejecting any culpability. Focusing on restoring their moral standing through these tactics, whites are able to avoid the challenge.[4]

One way that whites protect their positions when challenged on race is to invoke the discourse of self-defense. Through this discourse, whites characterize themselves as victimized, slammed, blamed, and attacked.[5] Whites who describe the interactions in this way are responding to the articulation of counternarratives alone; no physical violence has ever occurred in any interracial discussion or training that I am aware of. These self-defense claims work on multiple levels. They identify the speakers as morally superior while obscuring the true power of their social positions. The claims blame others with less social power for their discomfort and falsely describe that discomfort as dangerous. The self-defense approach also reinscribes racist imagery. By positioning themselves as the victim of antiracist efforts, they cannot be the beneficiaries of whiteness. Claiming that it is they who have been unfairly treated—through a challenge to their position or an expectation that they listen to the perspectives and experiences of people of color—they can demand that more social resources (such as time and attention) be channeled in their direction to help them cope with this mistreatment.

When I consult with organizations that want me to help them recruit and retain a more diverse workforce, I am consistently warned that past efforts to address the lack of diversity have resulted in trauma for white employees. This is literally the term used to describe the impact of a brief and isolated workshop: *trauma*. This trauma has required years of avoiding the topic altogether, and although the business leaders feel they are ready to begin again, I am cautioned to proceed slowly and be careful. Of course, this white racial trauma in response to equity efforts has also ensured that the organization has remained overwhelmingly white.

The language of violence that many whites use to describe antiracist endeavors is not without significance, as it is another example of how white fragility distorts reality. By employing terms that connote physical abuse, whites tap into the classic story that people of color (particularly African Americans) are dangerous and violent. In so doing, whites distort the real direction of danger between whites and others. This history becomes profoundly minimized when whites claim they don't feel safe or are under attack when they find themselves in the rare situation of merely talking about race with people of color. The use of this language of violence illustrates how fragile and ill-equipped most white people are to confront racial tensions, and their subsequent projection of this tension onto people of color.[6]

Sociologist Eduardo Bonilla-Silva, in his study of color-blind racism, describes an aspect of white fragility: "Because the new racial climate in America forbids the open expression of racially based feelings, views, and positions, when whites discuss issues that make them uncomfortable, they become almost incomprehensible."[7] Probing forbidden racial issues results in verbal incoherence—digressions, long pauses, repetition, and self-corrections. Bonilla-Silva suggests that this incoherent talk is a function of talking about race in a world that insists that race does not matter. This incoherence suggests that many white people are unprepared to explore, even on a preliminary level, their racial perspectives and to work to shift their understanding of racism. This reluctance maintains white power because the ability to determine which narratives are authorized and which are suppressed is the foundation of cultural domination. This reluctance has further implications, for if whites cannot explore alternate racial perspectives, they can only reinscribe white perspectives as universal.

However, whites do engage in racial discourse under controlled conditions. We notice the racial positions of racial others and discuss this freely among ourselves, albeit often in coded ways. The refusal to directly acknowledge this race talk results in a kind of split consciousness that leads to irrationality and incoherence. This denial also guarantees that the racial misinformation that circulates in the culture and frames our perspectives will be left unexamined. The continual retreat from the discomfort of authentic racial engagement in a culture in which racial disparity is infused limits white people's ability to form authentic connections across racial lines and perpetuates a cycle that keeps racism in place.

A cogent example of white fragility occurred during a workplace anti-racism training I co-facilitated with an inter-racial team. One of the white participants left the session and went back to her desk, upset at receiving (what appeared to the training team as) sensitive and diplomatic feedback on how some of her statements had impacted several of the people of color in the room. At break, several other white participants approached me and my fellow trainers and reported that they had talked to the woman at her desk, and that she was very upset that her statements had been challenged. (Of course, "challenged" was not how she phrased her concern. It was framed as her being "falsely accused" of having a racist impact.) Her friends wanted to alert us to the fact that she was in poor health and "might be having a heart-attack." Upon questioning from us, they clarified that they meant this literally. These coworkers were sincere in their fear that the young woman might actually die as a result of the feedback. Of course when news of the women's potentially fatal condition reached the rest of the participant group, all attention was immediately focused back onto her and away from engagement with the impact she had had on the people of color. As professor of social work Rich Vodde states, "If privilege is defined as a legitimization of one's entitlement to resources, it can also be defined as permission to escape or avoid any challenges to this entitlement."[8]

White equilibrium is a cocoon of racial comfort, centrality, superiority, entitlement, racial apathy, and obliviousness, all rooted in an identity of being good people free of racism. Challenging this cocoon throws off our racial balance. Because being racially off balance is so rare, we have not had to build the capacity to sustain the discomfort. Thus, whites find these challenges unbearable and want them to stop.

WHITE FRAGILITY AS A FORM OF BULLYING

Let me be clear: while the capacity for white people to sustain challenges to our racial positions is limited—and, in this way, fragile—the effects of our responses are not fragile at all; they are quite powerful because they take advantage of historical and institutional power and control. We wield this power and control in whatever way is most useful in the moment to protect our positions. If we need to cry so that all the resources rush back to us and attention is diverted away from a discussion of our racism, then we will cry (a strategy most commonly employed by white middle-class women). If we need to take umbrage and respond with righteous outrage, then we will take umbrage. If we need to argue, minimize, explain, play devil's advocate, pout, tune out, or withdraw to stop the challenge, then we will.

White fragility functions as a form of bullying; I am going to make it so miserable for you to confront me—no matter how diplomatically you try to do so—that you will simply back off, give up, and never raise the issue again. White fragility keeps people of color in line and "in their place." In this way, it is a powerful form of white racial control. Social power is not fixed; it is constantly challenged and needs to be maintained. We might think of the triggers of white fragility discussed in chapter 7 as challenges to white power and control, and of white fragility as the means to end the challenge and maintain that power and control.

Let me also be clear that the term "white fragility" is intended to describe a very specific white phenomenon. White fragility is much more than mere defensiveness or whining. It may be conceptualized as the *sociology of dominance*: an outcome of white people's socialization into white supremacy and a means to protect, maintain, and reproduce white supremacy. The term is *not applicable* to other groups who may register complaints or otherwise be deemed difficult (e.g., "student fragility").

In my workshops, I often ask people of color, "How often have you given white people feedback on our unaware yet inevitable racism? How often has that gone well for you?" Eye-rolling, head-shaking, and outright laughter follow, along with the consensus of *rarely, if ever*. I then ask, "What would it be like if you could simply give us feedback, have us graciously receive it, reflect, and work to change the behavior?" Recently a man of color sighed and said, "It would be revolutionary." I ask my fellow whites to consider the profundity of that response. It would be *revolutionary* if we could receive, reflect, and work to change the behavior. On the one hand, the man's response points to how difficult and fragile we are. But on the other hand, it indicates how simple it can be to take responsibility for our racism. However, we aren't likely to get there if we are operating from the dominant worldview that only intentionally mean people can participate in racism.

CHAPTER 9

WHITE FRAGILITY IN ACTION

A board president has finally obtained agreement from the school to sponsor racial equity training for his predominately white teaching staff. But when he hears the workshop's title, he backs away, not liking that the term white is used.

When I was a professor of education, my university was situated ten miles from a city that is roughly 56 percent black and Latinx. Our student population was 97 percent white, and many of them did their internships in the public schools in this city. My department hadn't hired a faculty member of color in seventeen years. I repeatedly brought this up as an issue, but silence repeatedly followed. Eventually, a white colleague came to my office and angrily told me, "Every time you bring this up, you are saying that we shouldn't have our jobs."

A white man works for an Indian tribe. He consistently lets the Native people he works with know how "exhausted" he is from "seeing injustice." He doesn't know how much longer he can endure the job. His Native coworkers feel pressured to repeatedly console him and encourage him to stay.

I receive a call from a virtually all-white organization that is interested in racial equity training. They want to know how I will ensure that the participants will feel comfortable.

I have just given a keynote talk on what it means to be white in a society that proclaims that being white means nothing, while remaining deeply separated and unequal by race. The focus of my talk is on how race shapes white identity and the inevitable patterns that result. A white woman who works with Native Americans approaches the event organizer, who is a woman of color. The white woman is furious. "What about Native Americans? You left out Native Americans!" She berates the organizer for several minutes at a volume that I can hear from across the stage. When I intervene, she is calmer but still chastises me for leaving out Native Americans—who are "the most oppressed of all." At no point does she acknowledge any aspect of the talk that relates to her as a white person, share any insight she may have gained into her own whiteness, or consider the impact of berating a woman of color who didn't actually give the talk.

As a former professor and current facilitator and consultant, I am in a position to give white people feedback on how their unintentional racism is manifesting itself. In this position, I have observed countless enactments of white fragility. One of the most common is outrage: "How dare you suggest that I could have said or done something racist!" Although these are unpleasant moments for me, they are also rather amusing. The reason I am there in the first place is because I have been hired specifically to do just that; I have been asked to help the members of the organization understand why their workplace continues to remain white, why they are having so much trouble recruiting people of color, and/or why the people of color they hire don't stay.

At this point in my career, I rarely encounter the kind of open hostility that I was met with in my early days as a facilitator. I attribute this change to the years of experience behind my pedagogy. Of course, I am also white, which makes other white people much more receptive to the message. I am often amazed at what I can say to groups of primarily white people. I can describe our culture as white supremacist and say things like "All white people are invested in and collude with racism" without my fellow white people running from the room or reeling from trauma. Naturally, I don't walk in and lead with those statements; I strategically guide people to a shared understanding of what I mean by those claims. My own whiteness coupled with experience and strategy puts white people's overall reception of me light-years beyond how I was received in the early days.

White people are receptive to my presentation as long as it remains abstract. The moment I name some racially problematic dynamic or action happening in the room *in the moment*—for example, "Sharon, may I give you some feedback? While I understand it wasn't intentional, your response to Jason's story invalidates his experience as a black man"— white fragility erupts. Sharon defensively explains that she was misunderstood and then angrily withdraws, while others run in to defend her by re-explaining "what she really meant." The point of the feedback is now lost, and hours must be spent repairing this perceived breach. And, of course, no one appears concerned about Jason. Shaking my head, I think to myself, "You asked me here to help you see your racism, but by god, I'd better not actually help you see your racism."

Throughout this book, I have attempted to make visible the inevitable racist assumptions held and patterns displayed by white people conditioned by living in a white supremacist culture. When these patterns are named or questioned, we have predictable responses. The responses begin with a set of unexamined assumptions, which, when questioned, trigger various emotions, which activate some expected behaviors. These behaviors are then justified by numerous claims. These responses, emotions, behaviors, and claims are illustrated in the following example of a recent eruption of white fragility.

I was co-leading a community workshop. Because an employer had not sponsored it, the participants had all voluntarily signed up and paid a fee to attend. For this reason, we could assume that they were open and interested in the content. I was working with a small group of white participants when a woman I will refer to as Eva stated that because she grew up in Germany, where she said there were no black people, she had learned nothing about race and held no racism. I pushed back on this claim by asking her to reflect on the messages she had received from her childhood about people who lived in Africa. Surely she was aware of Africa and had some impressions of the people there? Had she ever watched American films? If so, what impression did she get about African Americans? I also asked her to reflect on what she had absorbed from living in the US for the last twenty-three years, whether she had any relationships with African Americans here, and if not, then why not.

We moved on and I forgot about the interaction until she approached me after the workshop ended. She was furious and said that she had been deeply offended by our exchange and did not "feel seen." "You made assumptions about me!" she said. I apologized and told her that I would never want her to feel unseen or invalidated. However, I also held to my challenge that growing up in Germany would not preclude her from absorbing problematic racial messages about black people. She countered by telling me that she had never even seen a black person "before the American soldiers came." And when they did come, "all the German women thought them so beautiful that they wanted to connect with them." This was her evidence that she held no racism. With an internal sigh of defeat, I gave up at that point and repeated my apology. We parted ways, but her anger was unabated.

A few months later, one of my cofacilitators contacted Eva to tell her about an upcoming workshop. Eva was apparently still angry. She replied that she would never again attend a workshop led by me. Notice that I did not tell Eva that she was racist or that her story was racist. But what I did do was challenge her self-image as someone exempt from racism. Paradoxically, Eva's anger that I did not take her claims at face value surfaced within the context of a volunteer workshop on racism, which she ostensibly attended to deepen her understanding of racism.

Let's start with the common emotional reactions that white people have (and that Eva demonstrated) when our assumptions and behaviors are challenged.

FEELINGS

· Singled out	· Insulted
· Attacked	· Judged
· Silenced	· Angry
· Shamed	· Scared
· Guilty	· Outraged
· Accused	

When we have these feelings, it is common to behave in the following ways, as Eva did:

BEHAVIORS

· Crying	· Denying
· Physically leaving	· Focusing on intentions
· Emotionally withdrawing	· Seeking absolution
· Arguing	· Avoiding

Given that these are strong emotions and reactions, they need to be justified. What claims do we make to justify these feelings and behaviors? Some of the following claims suggest that the claimant has been falsely accused. Others suggest that the claimant is beyond the discussion ("I already know all this"). But all of them exempt the person from further engagement or accountability, as Eva's claims exempted her.

CLAIMS

· I know people of color.	· The real oppression is class [or gender, or anything other than race].
· I marched in the sixties.	
· I already know all this.	
· You are judging me.	· You are elitist.
· You don't know me.	· I just said one little innocent thing.
· You are generalizing.	
· That is just your opinion.	· Some people find offense where there is none.
· I disagree.	

- You don't do this the right way.
- You're playing the race card.
- This is not welcoming to me.
- You're being racist against me.
- You are making me feel guilty.
- You hurt my feelings.

- You misunderstood me.
- I don't feel safe.
- The problem is your tone.
- I can't say anything right.
- That was not my intention.
- I have suffered too.

Several of these claims are also made in an email I received through my public website; the following comments are partly excerpted and summarized (caps in original email). The writer opens by saying that according to her assessment of my age, I did not live through the things that she lived through, and therefore, "I seriously doubt that there is one single thing you could tell me about race." She goes on to state her credentials—how she lived through the momentous events of the civil rights movement, studied race and gender in college, is familiar with many famous black feminist writers and black politicians, and has known many black people throughout her life: neighbors, classmates, and colleagues. Further, the author suffers from the same illness that a black friend's sister died from decades earlier. This shared illness appears to be further proof of her alliance with black people. She uses these experiences and relationships as evidence that she has been able to shed any racism she may have had: "All the things you say whites 'absorb'? I got them wrung out of me through my life and my education." Her next move takes race off the table and replaces it with an oppression she experiences, sexism: "No, I don't want to talk about race any more. I want to talk about GENDER." She ends by closing down any further engagement, saying that she likely wouldn't read any email I would send her.

I am confident that some of the feelings, behaviors, and claims illustrated in this email message will be familiar to white readers; we have either made some version of them ourselves or have heard others make them. Yet as with so many aspects of racism, we rarely examine or consider them problematic. So let's go under the surface and examine the framework of assumptions many of these claims rest on.

ASSUMPTIONS

- Racism is simply personal prejudice.
- I am free of racism.
- I will be the judge of whether racism has occurred.
- My learning is finished; I know all I need to know.
- Racism can only be intentional; my not having intended racism cancels out the impact of my behavior.
- My suffering relieves me of racism or racial privilege.
- White people who experience another form of oppression cannot experience racial privilege.
- If I am a good person, I can't be racist.
- I am entitled to remain comfortable/have this conversation the way I want to.
- How I am perceived by others is the most important issue.
- As a white person, I know the best way to challenge racism.
- If I am feeling challenged, you are doing this wrong.
- It's unkind to point out racism.
- Racism is conscious bias. I have none, so I am not racist.
- Racists are bad individuals, so you are saying that I am a bad person.
- If you knew me or understood me, you would know I can't be racist.
- I have friends of color, so I can't be racist.
- There is no problem; society is fine the way it is.
- Racism is a simple problem. People just need to . . .
- My worldview is objective and the only one operating.
- If I can't see it, it isn't legitimate.
- If you have more knowledge on the subject than I do, you think you're better than me.

Now that we have identified the underlying assumptions that engender these feelings, behaviors, and claims, let's consider how they function.

FUNCTIONS OF WHITE FRAGILITY

- Maintain white solidarity
- Close off self-reflection
- Trivialize the reality of racism
- Silence the discussion
- Make white people the victims
- Hijack the conversation
- Protect a limited worldview
- Take race off the table
- Protect white privilege
- Focus on the messenger, not the message
- Rally more resources to white people

These behaviors and the assumptions undergirding them do not in fact present the claimant as racially open; quite the opposite. They block any entry point for reflection and engagement. Further, they block the ability to repair a racial breach. They fan racial divisions as they seethe with hostility and resentment. In summary, the prevailing white racial assumptions and the behaviors they engender protect racism.

CHAPTER 10

WHITE FRAGILITY AND THE RULES OF ENGAGEMENT

Given the dominant conceptualization of racism as individual acts of cruelty, it follows that only terrible people who consciously don't like people of color can enact racism. Though this conceptualization is misinformed, it is not benign. In fact, it functions beautifully to make it nearly impossible to engage in the necessary dialogue and self-reflection that can lead to change. Outrage at the suggestion of racism is often followed by righteous indignation about the manner in which the feedback was given. After years of working with my fellow whites, I have discovered (as, I am sure, have countless people of color) a set of unspoken rules for how to give white people feedback on our inevitable and often unconscious racist assumptions and patterns. I have found that the only way to give feedback without triggering white fragility is not to give it at all. Thus, the first rule is cardinal:

1. Do not give me feedback on my racism under any circumstances.

If you insist on breaking the cardinal rule, then you must follow these other rules:

2. Proper tone is crucial—feedback must be given calmly. If any emotion is displayed, the feedback is invalid and can be dismissed.

3. There must be trust between us. You must trust that I am in no way racist before you can give me feedback on my racism.

4. Our relationship must be issue-free—if there are issues between us, you cannot give me feedback on racism until these unrelated issues are resolved.

5. Feedback must be given immediately. If you wait too long, the feedback will be discounted because it was not given sooner.

6. You must give feedback privately, regardless of whether the incident occurred in front of other people. To give feedback in front of any others who were involved in the situation is to commit a serious social transgression. If you cannot protect me from embarrassment, the feedback is invalid, and you are the transgressor.

7. You must be as indirect as possible. Directness is insensitive and will invalidate the feedback and require repair.

8. As a white person, I must feel completely safe during any discussion of race. Suggesting that I have racist assumptions or patterns will cause me to feel unsafe, so you will need to rebuild my trust by never giving me feedback again. Point of clarification: when I say "safe," what I really mean is "comfortable."

9. Highlighting my racial privilege invalidates the form of oppression that *I* experience (e.g., classism, sexism, heterosexism, ageism, ableism, transphobia). We will then need to turn our attention to how *you* oppressed *me*.

10. You must acknowledge my intentions (always good) and agree that my good intentions cancel out the impact of my behavior.

11. To suggest my behavior had a racist impact is to have misunderstood me. You will need to allow me to explain myself until you can acknowledge that it was *your* misunderstanding.

The contradictions in these rules are irrelevant; their function is to obscure racism, protect white dominance, and regain white equilibrium. And they do so very effectively. Yet from an understanding of racism as a system of unequal institutional power, we need to ask ourselves where these rules come from and whom they serve.

Many of us actively working to interrupt racism continually hear complaints about the "gotcha" culture of white antiracism. We are sometimes depicted as looking for every incident we can find so we can spring out, point our fingers, and shout, "You're a racist!" While certainly some white people arrogantly set themselves apart from other whites by acting in this way, in my experience, this is not the norm. It is far more common for sincere white people to agonize over when and how to give feedback to a fellow white person, given the ubiquity of white fragility. White fragility punishes the person giving feedback and presses them back into silence. It also maintains white solidarity—the tacit agreement that we will protect white privilege and not hold each other accountable for our racism. When the individual giving the feedback is a person of color, the charge is "playing the race card," and the consequences of white fragility are much more penalizing.

Racism is the norm rather than an aberration. Feedback is key to our ability to recognize and repair our inevitable and often unaware collusion. In recognition of this, I try to follow these guidelines:

1. How, where, and when you give me feedback is irrelevant—it is the feedback I want and need. Understanding that it is hard to give, I will take it any way I can get it. From my position of social, cultural, and institutional white power and privilege, I am perfectly safe and I can handle it. If I cannot handle it, *it's on me* to build my racial stamina.
2. Thank you.

The above guidelines rest on the understanding that there is no face to save and the game is up; I know that I have blind spots and unconscious investments in racism. My investments are reinforced every day in mainstream society. I did not set this system up, but it does unfairly benefit me, I do use it to my advantage, and I am responsible for interrupting it. I need to work hard to change my role in this system, but I can't do it alone. This understanding leads me to gratitude when others help me.

White fragility is also evidenced in the need for so many white progressives to "build trust" before they can explore racism in workshops, support groups, and other educational forums. Many who are involved in racial justice education will recognize this white call for racial trust, which surfaces in a variety of ways: facilitators devoting time to exercises intended to build trust, creating ground rules and guidelines to engender trust, and participant justifications for non-engagement (e.g., "I am not going to share, because I don't feel trust here."). I have asked many colleagues just exactly what my fellow white people mean by the call for trust. I am confident the need for trust does not relate to having your wallet stolen or being physically assaulted, although at a subconscious level, that very well may be what is at play when the group is racially mixed, given the power of implicit bias and the relentless racist conditioning whites receive. Still, I believe that what it comes down to is this: I need to trust that you won't think I am racist before I can work on my racism.

Consider the following common guidelines that have "building trust" at their base:

- *Don't judge*: Refraining from judgment is not humanly possible, so this guideline cannot be achieved or enforced and is functionally meaningless.
- *Don't make assumptions*: The nature of an assumption is that you don't know you are making it, so this guideline cannot be achieved or enforced and is functionally meaningless.
- *Assume good intentions*: By emphasizing intentions over impact, this guideline privileges the intentions of the aggressor over the impact of their behavior on the target. In so doing, the aggressor's intentions become the most important issue. In essence, this guideline tells victims that as long as there was no intention to cause harm, they need to let go of the hurt and move on. In so

doing, this guideline upholds white racial innocence while minimizing the impact of racism on people of color.

- *Speak your truth*: The admonition to speak the truth seems to be an unnecessary guideline. I have not seen a pattern of lying in these groups. Have I seen defensiveness, distancing behavior, silence, avoidance of taking risks? Yes. But have I observed people not speaking their truth? No. More importantly, what if your truth is that you are color blind? Because no one can actually be color blind in a racist society, the claim that you are color blind is not a truth; it is a false belief. Yet this guideline can position all beliefs as truths and, as such, equally valid. Given that the goal of antiracist work is to identify and challenge racism and *the misinformation that supports it*, all perspectives are *not* equally valid; some are rooted in racist ideology and need to be uncovered and challenged. We must distinguish between sharing your beliefs so that we can identify how they may be upholding racism and stating your beliefs as "truths" that cannot be challenged.

- *Respect*: The problem with this guideline is that respect is rarely defined, and what feels respectful to white people can be exactly what does not create a respectful environment for people of color. For example, white people often define as respectful an environment with no conflict, no expression of strong emotion, no challenging of racist patterns, and a focus on intentions over impact. But such an atmosphere is exactly what creates an inauthentic, white-norm-centered, and thus hostile environment for people of color.

The unexamined assumption underlying these guidelines is that they can be universally applied. But because they do not account for unequal power relations, they do not function the same way across race. These guidelines are primarily driven by white fragility, and they are accommodations made to coddle white fragility. The very conditions that most white people insist on to remain comfortable are those that support the racial status quo (white centrality, dominance, and professed innocence). For people of color, the racial status quo is hostile and needs to be interrupted, not reinforced. The essential message of trust is *be nice*. And according to dominant white norms, the suggestion that someone is racist is not "nice."

Guidelines such as those above can also be turned against people of color. "If you challenge my racial patterns, then you are assuming that what I did was rooted in racism, and you shouldn't make assumptions." Or, "You are denying my truth that race has nothing to do with my actions." Now *you* are the transgressor. These conditions reproduce the weight of racism that people of color must constantly carry: putting aside their own needs to focus on white needs. An antidote to white fragility is to build up our stamina to bear witness to the pain of racism that we cause, not to impose conditions that require people of color to continually validate our denial.

Of course, we would ideally guide each other in this work with compassion; it is much easier to look at something unwanted within ourselves if we don't feel judged or criticized. But what if someone does literally point a finger and boldly say, "You are racist!"? (This accusation is a deep fear of progressive whites.) It is still on me to identify my racist patterns and work to change them. If the point being made is aimed at that goal, then regardless of how carefully or indirectly it is being made, I need to focus on the overall point. The method of delivery cannot be used to delegitimize what is being illuminated or as an excuse for disengagement.

To let go of the messenger and focus on the message is an advanced skill and is especially difficult to practice if someone comes at us with a self-righteous tone. If kindness gets us there faster, I am all for it. But I do not require anything from someone giving me feedback before I can engage with that feedback. Part of my processing of that feedback will be to separate it from its delivery and ascertain the central point and its contribution to my growth. Many of us are not there yet, but this is what we need to work toward. I have been in many white racial justice groups wherein the participants expended much energy making sure people were kind and compassionate to each other and didn't "break trust." So much energy, in fact, that we could no longer help each other see our problematic patterns without breaking the norms of the group. So unless that kindness is combined with clarity and the courage to name and challenge racism, this approach protects white fragility and needs to be challenged.

As I have tried to show throughout this book, white people raised in Western society are conditioned into a white supremacist worldview because it is the bedrock of our society and its institutions. Regardless of whether a parent told you that everyone was equal, or the poster in the hall of your white suburban school proclaimed the value of diversity, or you have traveled abroad, or you have people of color in your workplace or family, the ubiquitous socializing power of white supremacy cannot be avoided. The messages circulate 24-7 and have little or nothing to do with intentions, awareness, or agreement. Entering the conversation with this understanding is freeing because it allows us to focus on *how*—rather than *if*—our racism is manifest. When we move beyond the good/bad binary, we can become eager to identify our racist patterns because interrupting those patterns becomes more important than managing how we think we look to others.

I repeat: stopping our racist patterns must be more important than working to convince others that we don't have them. We do have them, and people of color already know we have them; our efforts to prove otherwise are not convincing. An honest accounting of these patterns is no small task given the power of white fragility and white solidarity, but it is necessary.

CHAPTER 11

WHITE WOMEN'S TEARS

But you are my sister, and I share your pain!

The term *white tears* refers to all the ways, both literally and metaphorically, that white fragility manifests itself through white people's laments over how hard racism is on *us*. In my work, I consistently encounter these tears in their various forms, and many writers have already provided excellent critiques.[1] Here, I want to address one manifestation of white tears: those shed by white women in cross-racial settings. The following example illustrates both the frustration that people of color feel with those tears and white women's sense of entitlement to freely shed them.

When another police shooting of an unarmed black man occurred, my workplace called for an informal lunch gathering of people who wanted to connect and find support. Just before the gathering, a woman of color pulled me aside and told me that she wanted to attend but she was "in no mood for white women's tears today." I assured her that I would handle it. As the meeting started, I told my fellow white participants that if they felt moved to tears, they should please leave the room. I would go with them for support, but I asked that they not cry in the mixed group. After the discussion, I spent the next hour explaining to a very outraged white woman why she was asked not to cry in the presence of the people of color.

I understand that expressing our heartfelt emotions—especially as they relate to racial injustices—is an important progressive value. To repress our feelings seems counterintuitive to being present, compassionate, and supportive. So why would my colleague of color make such a request? In short, white women's tears have a powerful impact in this setting, effectively reinscribing rather than ameliorating racism.

Many of us see emotions as naturally occurring. But emotions are political in two key ways. First, our emotions are shaped by our biases and beliefs, our cultural frameworks. For example, if I believe—consciously or unconsciously—that it is normal and appropriate for men to express anger but not women, I will have very different emotional responses to men's and women's expressions of anger. I might see a man who expresses anger as competent and in charge and may feel respect for him, while I see a woman who expresses anger as childish and out of control and may feel contempt for her. If I believe that only bad people are racist, I will feel hurt, offended, and shamed when an unaware racist assumption of mine is pointed out. If I instead believe that having racist assumptions is inevitable (but possible to change), I will feel gratitude when an unaware racist assumption is pointed out; now I am aware of and can change that assumption. In this way, emotions are not natural; they are the result of the frameworks we are using to make sense of social relations. And of course, social relations are political. Our emotions are also political because they are often externalized; our emotions drive behaviors that impact other people.

White women's tears in cross-racial interactions are problematic for several reasons connected to how they impact others. For example, there is a long historical backdrop of black men being tortured and murdered because of a white woman's distress, and we white women bring these histories with us. Our tears trigger the terrorism of this history, particularly for African Americans. A cogent and devastating example is Emmett Till, a fourteen-year-old boy who reportedly flirted with a white woman—Carolyn Bryant—in a grocery store in Mississippi in 1955. She reported this alleged flirtation to her husband, Roy Bryant, and a few days later, Roy and his half-brother, J. W. Milam, lynched Till, abducting him from his great-uncle's home. They beat him to death, mutilated his body, and sank him in the Tallahatchie River. An all-white jury acquitted the men, who later admitted to the murder. On her deathbed, in 2017, Carolyn Bryant recanted this story and admitted that she had lied. The murder of Emmett Till is just one example of the history that informs an oft-repeated warning from my African American colleagues: "When a white woman cries, a black man gets hurt." Not knowing or being sensitive to this history is another example of white centrality, individualism, and lack of racial humility.

Because of its seeming innocence, well-meaning white women crying in cross-racial interactions is one of the more pernicious enactments of white fragility. The reasons we cry in these interactions vary. Perhaps we were given feedback on our racism. Not understanding that unaware white racism is inevitable, we hear the feedback as a moral judgment, and our feelings are hurt. A classic example occurred in a workshop I was co-leading. A black man who was struggling to express a point referred to himself as stupid. My co-facilitator, a black woman, gently countered that he was not stupid but that society would have him believe that he was. As she was explaining the power of internalized racism, a white woman interrupted with, "What he was trying to say was . . ." When my co-facilitator pointed out that the white woman had reinforced the racist idea that she could best speak for a black man, the woman erupted in tears. The training came to a complete halt as most of the room rushed to comfort her and angrily accuse the black facilitator of unfairness. (Even though the participants were there to learn how racism works, how dare the facilitator point out an example of how racism works!) Meanwhile, the black man she had spoken for was left alone to watch her receive comfort.

A colleague of color shared an example in which a white woman—new to a racial justice organization—was offered a full-time position as the supervisor of the women of color who had worked there for years and had trained her. When the promotion was announced, the white woman tearfully requested support from the women of color as she embarked on her new learning curve. The new supervisor probably saw her tears as an expression of humility about the limits of her racial knowledge and expected support to follow. The women of color had to deal with the injustice of the promotion, the invalidation of their abilities, and the lack of racial awareness of the white person now in charge of their livelihoods. While trying to manage their own emotional reactions, they were put on the spot; if they did not make some comforting gesture, they risked being viewed as angry and insensitive.

Whether intended or not, when a white woman cries over some aspect of racism, all the attention immediately goes to her, demanding time, energy, and attention from everyone in the room when they should be focused on ameliorating racism. While she is given attention, the people of color are yet again abandoned and/or blamed. As Stacey Patton, an assistant professor of multimedia journalism at Morgan State University's School of Global Journalism and Communication, states in her critique of white women's tears, "then comes the waiting for us to comfort and reassure them that they're not bad people."[2] Antiracism strategist and facilitator Reagen Price paraphrases an analogy based on the work of critical race scholar Kimberlé Crenshaw. Price says, "Imagine first responders at the scene of an accident rushing to comfort the person whose car struck a pedestrian, while the pedestrian lies bleeding on the street." In a common but particularly subversive move, racism becomes about white distress, white suffering, and white victimization.

White men, of course, are also racially fragile, but I have not seen their fragility manifest itself in cross-racial discussions as actual crying. Their fragility most commonly shows up as varying forms of dominance and intimidation, including these:

· Control of the conversation by speaking first, last, and most often
· Arrogant and disingenuous invalidation of racial inequality via "just playing the devil's advocate"
· Simplistic and presumptuous proclamations of "the answer" to racism ("People just need to . . .")

- Playing the outraged victim of "reverse racism"
- Accusations that the legendary "race card" is being played
- Silence and withdrawal
- Hostile body language
- Channel-switching ("The true oppression is class!")
- Intellectualizing and distancing ("I recommend this book . . .")
- "Correcting" the racial analysis of people of color and white women
- Pompously explaining away racism and the experiences of people of color

All these moves push race off the table, help white men retain control of the discussion, end the challenge to their positions, and reassert their dominance.

Because racism does not rely solely on individual actors, the racist system is reproduced automatically. To interrupt it, we need to recognize and challenge the norms, structures, and institutions that keep it in place. But because they benefit us, racially inequitable relations are comfortable for most white people. Consequently, if we whites want to interrupt this system, we have to get racially *uncomfortable* and be willing to examine the effects of our racial engagement. This includes not indulging in whatever reactions we have—anger, defensiveness, self-pity, and so forth—in a given cross-racial encounter without first reflecting on what is driving our reactions and how they will affect other people.

Tears that are driven by white guilt are self-indulgent. When we are mired in guilt, we are narcissistic and ineffective; guilt functions as an excuse for inaction. Further, because we so seldom have authentic and sustained cross-racial relationships, our tears do not feel like solidarity to people of color we have not previously supported. Instead, our tears function as impotent reflexes that don't lead to constructive action. We need to reflect on when we cry and when we don't, and why. In other words, what does it take to move us? Since many of us have not learned how racism works and our role in it, our tears may come from shock and distress about what we didn't know or recognize. For people of color, our tears demonstrate our racial insulation and privilege.

I asked the woman of color I refer to in the opening of this chapter if I was missing anything in this list. This is her response:

> It's infuriating because of its audacity of disrespect to our experience. You are crying because you are uncomfortable with your feelings when we are barely allowed to have any. You are ashamed or some such thing and cry, but we are not allowed to have any feelings because then we are being difficult. We are supposed to remain stoic and strong because otherwise we become the angry and scary people of color. We are only allowed to have feelings for the sake of your entertainment, as in the presentation of our funerals. And even then, there are expectations of what is allowed for us to express. We are abused daily, beaten, raped, and killed but you are sad and that's what is important. That's why it is sooooo hard to take.

I have certainly been moved to tears by someone's story in cross-racial discussions. And I imagine that sometimes tears are appreciated, as they can validate and bear witness to the pain of racism for people of color. But I try to be very thoughtful about how and when I cry. I try to cry quietly so that I don't take up more space, and if people rush to comfort me, I do not accept the comfort; I let them know that I am fine so we can move on.

THE MEN WHO LOVE US

In addition to the general dynamics discussed thus far, white women's tears in cross-racial discussions have a very specific effect on men. I have seen our tears manipulate men of all races, but the consequences of this manipulation are not the same. White men occupy the highest positions in the race and gender hierarchy. Thus, they have the power to define their own reality and that of others. This reality includes not only whose experiences are valid, but *who* is fundamentally valid. In the white racial frame, not all women are deemed worthy of recognition. For example, contrary to popular white mythology, white women—not people of color—have been the primary beneficiaries of affirmative action. When forced to do so, white men could acknowledge white women's humanity; white women were their sisters, wives, and daughters. And of course, through these relationships, white women's increased access to resources benefited white men. This humanity has yet to be granted to women of color.

White men also get to authorize what constitutes pain and whose pain is legitimate. When white men come to the rescue of white women in cross-racial settings, patriarchy is reinforced as they play savior to our damsel in distress. By legitimating white women as the targets of harm, both white men and women accrue social capital. People of color are abandoned and left to bear witness as the resources meted out to white people actually increase—yet again—on their backs.

Men of color may also come to the aid of white women in these exchanges and may also be driven by their conditioning under sexism and patriarchy. But men of color have the additional weight of racism to navigate. This weight has historically been deadly. For black men in particular, the specter of Till and countless others who have been beaten and killed over a white woman's claims of cross-racial distress is ever present. Ameliorating a white woman's distress as quickly as possible may be felt as a literal matter of survival. Yet coming to the rescue of a white woman also drives a wedge between men and women of color. Rather than receive social capital that reinforces his status, a man of color put in this position must now live with the agony of having to support a white woman over a person of color in order to survive.

White people do need to feel grief about the brutality of white supremacy and our role in it. In fact, our numbness to the racial injustice that occurs daily is key to holding it in place. But our grief must lead to sustained and transformative action. Because our emotions are indicators of our internal frameworks, they can serve as entry points into the deeper self-awareness that leads to this action. Examining what is at the root of our emotions (shame for not knowing, guilt for hurting someone, hurt feelings because we think we must have been misunderstood) will enable us to address these frameworks. We also need to examine our responses toward other people's emotions and how they may reinscribe race and gender hierarchies. Our racial socialization sets us up to repeat racist behavior, regardless of our intentions or self-image. We must continue to ask *how* our racism manifests, not *if*.

CHAPTER 12

WHERE DO WE GO FROM HERE?

The equity team has been invited to a meeting with the company's new web developer. The team consists of two women, both of whom are black, and me. The new web developer, who is also black, wants to interview us so that she can build our page. She starts the meeting by giving us a survey to fill out. Many questions on the survey inquire about our intended audience, methods, goals, and objectives. I find the questions tedious and feel irritated by them. Pushing the survey aside, I try to explain verbally. I tell the web developer that we go out into the satellite offices to facilitate antiracism training. I add that the training is not always well received; in fact, one member of our team was told not to come back. I make a joke: "The white people were scared by Deborah's hair" (Deborah is black and has long locked braids). The meeting ends and we move on.

A few days later, one of my team members lets me know that the web developer—who I will call Angela—was offended by my hair comment. While I wasn't paying attention at the time, once I am informed, I quickly realize why that comment was off. I seek out a friend who is white and has a solid understanding of cross-racial dynamics. We discuss my feelings (embarrassment, shame, guilt) and then she helps me identify the various ways my racism was revealed in that interaction. After this processing, I feel ready to repair the relationship. I ask Angela to meet with me, and she accepts.

I open by asking Angela, "Would you be willing to grant me the opportunity to repair the racism I perpetrated toward you in that meeting?" When she agrees, I continue. "I realize that my comment about Deborah's hair was inappropriate."

Angela nods and explains that she did not know me and did not want to be joking about black women's hair (a sensitive issue for many black women) with a white woman whom she did not have a trusting relationship with, much less in a professional work meeting.

I apologize and ask her if I have missed anything else problematic in the meeting.

"Yes," she replies. "That survey? I wrote that survey. And I have spent my life justifying my intelligence to white people."

My chest constricts as I immediately realize the impact of my glib dismissal of the survey. I acknowledge this impact and apologize.

She accepts my apology. I ask Angela if there is anything else that needs to be said or heard so that we may move forward.

She replies that yes, there is. "The next time you do something like this, would you like feedback publicly or privately?" she asks.

I answer that given my role as an educator, I would appreciate receiving the feedback publicly as it is important for white people to see that I am also engaged in a lifelong process of learning and growth. And I could model for other white people how to receive feedback openly and without defensiveness.

She tells me that although these dynamics occur daily between white people and people of color, my willingness to repair doesn't, and that she appreciates this. We move on.

In chapter 9, I identified the common emotions, behaviors, claims, and underlying assumptions of white fragility. In this chapter, we'll see how those elements would change if we transformed our racial paradigm.

It is difficult for me to imagine that my aforementioned interaction with Angela would have been as constructive if it had occurred before I began this work. I simply could not and would not have responded well if I had been operating from the dominant paradigm. When my coworker let me know that Angela was offended, I would have been filled with anxiety and immediately explained my intentions to my co-worker, seeking her understanding and absolution. I would have felt unfairly accused and seen myself as the victim of Angela's unfairness. In responding this way, I would have lost any potential relationship with her, protected my limited worldview, and stunted my emotional and intellectual growth. Yet day in and day out, this defensive reaction is what people of color get from white people, and it explains why they more often than not don't even try talking to us.

However, from a transformed paradigm, when we are given feed-back on our inevitable but unaware racist patterns, we might have very different feelings:

- Gratitude
- Excitement
- Discomfort
- Guilt
- Motivation
- Humility
- Compassion
- Interest

When we have these feelings, we might engage in the following behaviors:

- Reflection
- Apology
- Listening
- Processing
- Seeking more understanding
- Grappling
- Engaging
- Believing

What claims might we make when we have these feelings and engage in these behaviors? Notice that none of the following claims characterize us as falsely accused or as beyond the discussion; these claims suggest openness and humility.

- I appreciate this feedback.
- This is very helpful.
- It's my responsibility to resist defensiveness and complacency.
- This is hard, but also stimulating and important.
- Oops!
- It is inevitable that I have this pattern. I want to change it.
- It's personal but not strictly personal.
- I will focus on the message and not the messenger.
- I need to build my capacity to endure discomfort and bear witness to the pain of racism.
- I have some work to do.

These feelings, behaviors, and claims will probably be less familiar to readers, as they are all too rare. But when our fundamental understanding of racism is transformed, so are our assumptions and resultant behaviors. Imagine the difference in our environment, interactions, norms, and policies if the following list described our assumptions:

- Being good or bad is not relevant.
- Racism is a multilayered system embedded in our culture.
- All of us are socialized into the system of racism.
- Racism cannot be avoided.
- Whites have blind spots on racism, and I have blind spots on racism.
- Racism is complex, and I don't have to understand every nuance of the feedback to validate that feedback.
- Whites are / I am unconsciously invested in racism.
- Bias is implicit and unconscious; I don't expect to be aware of mine without a lot of ongoing effort.
- Giving us white people feedback on our racism is risky for people of color, so we can consider the feedback a sign of trust.

- Feedback on white racism is difficult to give; how I am given the feedback is not as relevant as the feedback itself.
- Authentic antiracism is rarely comfortable. Discomfort is key to my growth and thus desirable.
- White comfort maintains the racial status quo, so discomfort is necessary and important.
- I must not confuse comfort with safety; as a white person, I am safe in discussions of racism.
- The antidote to guilt is action.
- It takes courage to break with white solidarity; how can I support those who do?
- I bring my group's history with me; history matters.
- Given my socialization, it is much more likely that I am the one who doesn't understand the issue.
- Nothing exempts me from the forces of racism.
- My analysis must be intersectional (a recognition that my other social identities—class, gender, ability—inform how I was socialized into the racial system).
- Racism hurts (even kills) people of color 24-7. Interrupting it is more important than my feelings, ego, or self-image.

These assumptions might interrupt racism in various ways, such as the following:

- Minimize our defensiveness.
- Demonstrate our vulnerability.
- Demonstrate our curiosity and humility.
- Allow for growth.
- Stretch our worldview.
- Ensure action.
- Demonstrate that we practice what we profess to value.
- Build authentic relationships and trust.
- Interrupt privilege-protecting comfort.
- Interrupt internalized superiority.

When white people ask me what to do about racism and white fragility, the first thing I ask is, "What has enabled you to be a full, educated, professional adult and not know what to do about racism?" It is a sincere question. How have we managed not to know, when the information is all around us? When people of color have been telling us for years? If we take that question seriously and map out all the ways we have come to not know what to do, we will have our guide before us. For example, if my answer is that I was not educated about racism, I know that I will have to get educated. If my answer is that I don't know people of color, I will need to build relationships. If it is because there are no people of color in my environment, I will need to get out of my comfort zone and change my environment; addressing racism is not without effort.

Next, I say, "Do whatever it takes for you to internalize the above assumptions." I believe that if we white people were truly coming from these assumptions, not only would our interpersonal relationships change, but so would our institutions. Our institutions would change because we would see to it that they did. But we simply cannot end racism from the current paradigm.

The final advice I offer is this: "Take the initiative and find out on your own." To break with the conditioning of whiteness—the conditioning that makes us apathetic about racism and prevents us from developing the skills we need to interrupt it—white people need to find out for themselves what they can do. There is so much excellent advice out there today—written by both people of color and white people. Search it out. Break with the apathy of whiteness, and demonstrate that you care enough to put in the effort.

As an analogy, imagine you go to the doctor, who tells you that you have an acoustic neuroma. Just as she is about to explain what that is and what your options are, she gets an emergency call and must rush off, abruptly ending your visit. What would you do? You would very likely go home, get on the internet, and read everything you could find on the subject. You might join a discussion group with people who had experience with the condition. Even if the doctor wasn't called away and she explained the condition and gave you some advice, you would probably still go home and do the research so that you would have more than one opinion on such an important—perhaps even a life-and-death—condition. Bottom line: you would care enough to get informed. So consider racism a matter of life and death (as it is for people of color), and do your homework.

THE REPAIR

Returning to the example of the racism I perpetrated toward my co-worker, we can see that I followed a series of steps. These steps are based on the preceding list of assumptions and behaviors (reflection, apology, etc.) presented above. First, once I was aware that I had behaved problematically, I took the time to process my reaction with another white person. It was not Angela's duty to take care of my feelings or feel pressure to reassure me. I was also careful to choose someone who I knew would hold me accountable, not someone who would insist that Angela was too sensitive. After I vented my feelings (embarrassment, guilt, shame, and regret), we did our best to identify how I had reinforced racism. I was then ready to return to Angela. I was clear and open about why I wanted to meet with her, and asked her if she would be willing to meet. I was prepared for her to say no; if I could not accept no for an answer, then I would not have been ready to make an authentic apology.

When Angela and I met, I owned my racism. I did not focus on my intentions but focused on the impact of my behavior and apologized for that impact. Nor did I use passive framing such as "*If* you were offended." (Apologies that start this way are subtle efforts to put the onus on the recipients of our racism. Indirectly, we are saying that the breach was not inherently offensive—many would not find it offensive at all—but if you were offended because of your extreme sensitivity, then we are sorry.) I simply admitted that my behavior was offensive. Recognizing that I, as a white person, as well as my white friend who had helped me process my feelings, would most likely not understand all the dynamics, I asked Angela what I had missed. She was willing to enlighten me further, and I accepted this additional feedback and apologized. I made a commitment to do better, and I closed by asking her if there was anything else that needed to be said or heard so that we might move forward.

We then did move forward. Today, we have more trust—not less—in our relationship than we did before this incident. While I regret that it came at a cost to Angela, it wasn't the end of the world. Many people of color have assured me that they will not give up on me despite my racist patterns; they expect that I will have racist behavior given the society that socialized me. What they are looking for is not perfection but the ability to talk about what happened, the ability to repair. Unfortunately, it is rare for white people to own and repair our inevitable patterns of racism. Thus, relationships with white people tend to be less authentic for people of color.

GOING FORWARD

In chapter 4, I warned readers not to depend on people of color for our racial education and explained why this dependency is problematic. Readers may have been left wondering how we would get this information if we don't ask people of color to give it to us. We can get it in several interconnected ways. We can seek out the information from books, websites, films, and other available sources. Many people of color *are* committed to teaching whites about racism (on their own terms) and have been offering this information to us for decades, if not centuries. It is our own lack of interest or motivation that has prevented us from receiving it.

We can also demand that we be given this information in schools and universities and that we not be required to take special, elective courses to be exposed to it. We can get involved with multiracial organizations and white organizations working for racial justice. And we can build authentic cross-racial relationships and be willing to watch, listen, and learn. Sometimes, within the context of these relationships, we can ask direct questions and ask for explicit information, but this is not always necessary. Simply by virtue of living an integrated life and paying attention, we will learn what we need to know.

Still, white people do have knowledge of aspects of race and racism, and we can easily unearth this knowledge with some minimal reflection. For example, we can reflect on messages we have received, privileges we enjoy, how we came to be socialized to feel superior (while denying that we feel this way), and how all of this may be manifesting in our lives.

When I began this work, I dreaded getting feedback from people of color on my racist patterns and assumptions. Now I welcome this feedback. Perhaps the most powerful lesson I have learned in terms of interrupting my own white fragility is that this feedback is a positive sign in the relationship. Of course, the feedback seldom feels good—I occasionally feel embarrassed or defensive. But I also understand that there is no way for me to avoid enacting problematic patterns, so if a person of color trusts me enough to take the risk and tell me, then I am doing well.

Many people of color have shared with me that they don't bother giving feedback to a white person if they think the individual is unwilling to accept it; they either endure the microaggressions or drift away from the relationship. They do not feel close to white people to whom they can't speak honestly about racism, and these relationships always have a degree of distance and inauthenticity. While we worry that if we have revealed our racism in any way, the people of color in our lives will give up on us, I have found the opposite to be true. When we engage with the feedback and seek to repair the breach, the relationship deepens. Trying to explain away our racism does not fool people of color or bring them closer.

Because I will never be completely free of racism or finished with my learning, what are some things I can do or remember when my white fragility surfaces? There are several constructive responses we can have in the moment:

- Breathe.
- Listen.

- Reflect.
- Return to the list of underlying assumptions in this chapter.
- Seek out someone with a stronger analysis if you feel confused.
- Take the time you need to process your feelings, but do return to the situation and the persons involved.

We can interrupt our white fragility and build our capacity to sustain cross-racial honesty by being willing to tolerate the discomfort associated with an honest appraisal and discussion of our internalized superiority and racial privilege. We can challenge our own racial reality by acknowledging ourselves as racial beings with a particular and limited perspective on race. We can attempt to understand the racial realities of people of color through authentic interaction rather than through the media or through unequal relationships. We can take action to address our own racism, the racism of other whites, and the racism embedded in our institutions. All these efforts will require that we continually challenge our own socialization and investments in racism and the misinformation we have learned about people of color. We can educate ourselves about the history of race relations in our country. We can follow the leadership on antiracism from people of color and work to build authentic cross-racial relationships. We can get involved in organizations working for racial justice. And most important, we must break the silence about race and racism with other white people.

THE QUESTION OF GUILT

Audre Lorde eloquently addressed her thoughts on white guilt at the National Women's Studies Association Conference in 1981:

> I cannot hide my anger to spare you guilt, nor hurt feelings, nor answering anger; for to do so insults and trivializes all our efforts. Guilt is not a response to anger; it is a response to one's own actions or lack of action. If it leads to change then it can be useful, since it is then no longer guilt but the beginning of knowledge. Yet all too often, guilt is just

another name for impotence, for defensiveness destructive of communication; it becomes a device to protect ignorance and the continuation of things the way they are, the ultimate protection for changelessness.[1]

I am sometimes asked whether my work reinforces and takes advantage of white guilt. But I don't see my efforts to uncover how race shapes my life as a matter of guilt. I know that because I was socialized as white in a racism-based society, I have a racist worldview, deep racial bias, racist patterns, and investments in the racist system that has elevated me. Still, I don't feel guilty about racism. I didn't chose this socialization, and it could not be avoided. But I am responsible for my role in it. To the degree that I have done my best in each moment to interrupt my participation, I can rest with a clearer conscience. But that clear conscience is not achieved by complacency or a sense that I have arrived.

Unlike heavy feelings such as guilt, the continuous work of identifying my internalized superiority and how it may be manifesting itself is incredibly liberating. When I start from the premise that *of course* I have been thoroughly socialized into the racist culture in which I was born, I no longer need to expend energy denying that fact. I am eager—even excited—to identify my inevitable collusion so that I can figure out how to stop colluding! Denial and the defensiveness that is needed to maintain it is exhausting.

A POSITIVE WHITE IDENTITY?

There are many approaches to antiracist work; one of them is to try to develop a positive white identity. Those who promote this approach often suggest we develop this positive identity by reclaiming the cultural heritage that was lost during assimilation into whiteness for European ethnics. However, a positive white identity is an impossible goal. White identity is inherently racist; white people do not exist outside the system of white supremacy. This does not mean that we should stop identifying as white and start claiming only to be Italian or Irish. To do so is to deny the reality of racism in the here and now, and this denial would simply be color-blind racism. Rather, I strive to be "less white." To be less white is to be less racially oppressive. This requires me to be more racially aware, to be better educated about racism, and to continually challenge racial certitude and arrogance. To be less white is to be open to, interested in, and compassionate toward the racial realities of people of color. I can build a wide range of authentic and sustained relationships across race and accept that I have racist patterns. And rather than be defensive about those patterns, I can be interested in seeing them more clearly so that I might ameliorate them. To be less white is to break with white silence and white solidarity, to stop privileging the comfort of white people over the pain of racism for people of color, to move past guilt and into action. These less oppressive patterns are active, not passive. Ultimately, I strive for a less white identity for my own liberation and sense of justice, not to save people of color.

A FEW STRATEGIES FOR WORKING TOGETHER

When I give a talk or workshop, the number one question I get from white participants is, "How do I tell so-and-so about their racism without triggering white fragility?" My first response to this question is, "How would I tell you about *your* racism without triggering *your* white fragility?" With this response, I am trying to point out the unspoken assumption that the person asking the question is not part of the problem. In other words, the question distances the participant from racism; it assumes that the questioner doesn't need feedback or doesn't struggle with his or her own white fragility. The person's question is not one of humility or self-reflection.

Having said that, I can offer a few strategies for trying to work with one another on our white fragility. First, I try to affirm a person's perspective before I share mine, and when I do share mine, I try to point the finger inward, not outward. For example, I might say, "I can understand why you feel that way. I have felt that way myself. However, because of my opportunity to work with people of color and hear their perspectives, I have come to understand . . ." I then share what I have come to understand with the emphasis on how this understanding relates to me. While this strategy is not guaranteed to lower defensiveness, it's difficult to argue with someone who has framed a response as her or his own personal insight.

I also give myself some time if I feel at a loss to respond in the moment. When we have an ongoing relationship with someone, it's fine to take some time and return to the issue later. With this strategy, we can then choose a time when we feel more prepared and sense that the other person is open. In this case, I might say, "Can I talk to you about something? I have been feeling uncomfortable about our interaction the other day but it has taken me a while to get clarity on why. I have a better sense now. Can we return to our conversation?" I then do my best to share my thoughts and feelings as calmly and concisely as possible. Ultimately, I let go of changing the other person. If someone gains insight from what I share, that is wonderful. But the objective that guides me is my own need to break with white solidarity, even when it's uncomfortable, which it almost always is. In the end, my actions are driven by my own need for integrity, not a need to correct or change someone else.

PEOPLE OF COLOR NAVIGATING WHITE FRAGILITY

People of color have occasionally asked me how to navigate white fragility. I so wish I had a simple formula to offer them! I want us to stop manifesting white fragility so that people of color don't have to ask this question. Still, besides the strategies discussed thus far, there is another approach that people of color may find useful. Whenever you—as a person of color—do not want to bear the burden of pointing out a white person's racism but do not want to let it go, you might ask a white person whom you trust to deal with it. While addressing white racism is rarely easy, white people can certainly bear the brunt of a hostile response less painfully than people of color can. There may even be a little less fragility because the intervention is coming from another white person. This strategy also helps a supportive white person demonstrate support and practice breaking with white solidarity.

Some people of color have told me that it is useful to know how they have colluded with my white fragility. In answering this question, I must first be clear that navigating white fragility is fundamentally a matter of survival for people of color. The consequences of white fragility include hours of agonizing as well as far more extreme consequences such as being seen as a threat and a troublemaker. These biased assessments often lead to job loss, stress-related illness, criminal charges, and institutionalization. To choose to survive in any way deemed necessary is thus an empowered choice. It is white people's responsibility to be less fragile; people of color don't need to twist themselves into knots trying to navigate us as painlessly as possible. Still, in helping people of color decide whether or how to interrupt white fragility, I can share some ways that I have noticed people of color enabling mine.

Because I am seen as somewhat more racially aware than other whites, people of color will often give me a pass. While this is certainly more comfortable for me, it doesn't hold me accountable or support my racial growth. I ask my friends of color to trust that I can handle their feedback, and then it's on me to demonstrate myself as worthy of that trust. Although I recognize the risk it takes, I would not have my current awareness if people of color had chosen to protect my feelings. Since my learning will never be finished, neither will the need to hold me accountable.

When a person of color gives me feedback that I consider unfair, I am tempted to go to another person of color for reassurance that I am a good person. This search for reassurance pressures people of color to align with me over one another by agreeing that I have been unfairly attacked. Empathy with people in distress creates a strong urge to comfort them, and in my search for this comfort, I am, consciously or not, taking advantage of this urge. But the search for reassurance from people of color is inappropriate. My need functions as a kind of divide-and-conquer wedge. Further, my quest for reassurance upholds racism by reinforcing the very idea that the feedback was an unfair attack and/or that there was a correct way to give it and the person of color in question has broken the rules of engagement. In essence, by complaining to one person of color about the unfairness of feedback from another person of color (no matter how diplomatically or indirectly I try to mask my complaint), I am pressuring a person of color to collude with my racism.

Equity consultant Devon Alexander shared with me what is perhaps the most pernicious form of pressure on people of color: the pressure to collude with white fragility by minimizing their racial experiences to accommodate white denial and defensiveness. In other words, they don't share their pain with us because we can't handle it. This accommodation requires a profoundly unfair degree of inauthenticity and silent endurance. In a vicious racial cycle, white fragility has functioned to keep people of color from challenging racism in order to avoid white wrath. In turn, not challenging white people on racism upholds the racial order and whites' position within that order.

IN CONCLUSION

The default of the current system is the reproduction of racial inequality; our institutions were designed to reproduce racial inequality and they do so with efficiency. Our schools are particularly effective at this task. To continue reproducing racial inequality, the system only needs white people to be really nice and carry on, smile at people of color, be friendly across race, and go to lunch together on occasion. I am not saying that you shouldn't be nice. I suppose it's better than being mean. But niceness is not courageous. Niceness will not get racism on the table and will not keep it on the table when everyone wants it off. In fact, bringing racism to white people's attention is often seen as *not* nice, and being perceived as not nice triggers white fragility.

Interrupting racism takes courage and intentionality; the interruption is by definition not passive or complacent. So in answer to the question "Where do we go from here?," I offer that we must never consider ourselves finished with our learning. Even if challenging all the racism and superiority we have internalized was quick and easy to do, our racism would be reinforced all over again just by virtue of living in the culture. I have been engaged in this work in a range of forms for many years, and I continue to receive feedback on my stubborn patterns and unexamined assumptions. It is a messy, lifelong process, but one that is necessary to align my professed values with my real actions. It is also deeply compelling and transformative.

RESOURCES FOR CONTINUING EDUCATION

This brief list cannot do justice to the scores of excellent resources available to anyone willing to take the initiative to seek them out; it is intended as an entry point.

BOOKS, ARTICLES, AND BLOGS

Alexander, Michelle. *The New Jim Crow: Mass Incarceration in the Age of Colorblindness*. New York: New Press, 2010.

Anderson, Carol. *White Rage: The Unspoken Truth of Our Racial Divide*. New York: Bloomsbury, 2016.

Biewen, John. *Seeing White*. Podcast bibliography. Center for Documentary Studies, Duke University, 2015. http://podcast.cdsporch.org/seeing-white/seeing-white-bibliography.

Bonilla-Silva, Eduardo. *Racism Without Racists: Color-Blind Racism and the Persistence of Racial Inequality in America*. 4th ed. Lanham, MD: Rowman & Littlefield, 2013. First published 2003.

Brown, Dee. *Bury My Heart at Wounded Knee*. New York: Open Road Media, 2012.

Coates, Ta-Nehisi. *Between the World and Me*. New York: Spiegel & Grau, 2015.

———. "The Case for Reparations." *Atlantic*, June 2014.

Dyson, Michael Eric. *Tears We Cannot Stop: A Sermon to a White America*. New York: St. Martin's Press, 2017.

Feagin, Joe R. *The White Racial Frame: Centuries of Racial Framing and Counter-Framing*. New York: Routledge, 2013.

Gaskins, Pearl Fuyo, ed. *What Are You? Voices of Mixed-Race Young People*. New York: Henry Holt & Co., 1999.

Irving, Debby. *Waking Up White: And Finding Myself in the Story of Race*. Boston: Elephant Room Press, 2014.

Kamenetz, Anya. "Resources for Educators to Use in the Wake of Charlottesville." *NPR*, August 14, 2017. https://www.npr.org/sections/ed/2017/08/14/543390148/resources-for-educators-to-use-the-wake-of-charlottesville.

Kendi, Ibram X. *Stamped from the Beginning*. New York: Nation Books, 2016.

Lee, Stacey. *Unraveling the "Model-Minority" Stereotype: Listening to Asian American Youth*. New York: Teachers College Press, 1996.

———. *Up Against Whiteness: Race, School, and Immigrant Youth*. New York: Teachers College Press, 2005).

Loewen, James W. *Lies My Teacher Told Me: Everything Your American History Textbook Got Wrong*, rev. ed. New York: New Press, 20018.

Menakem, Resmaa. *My Grandmother's Hands: Racialized Trauma and the Pathway to Mending Our Hearts and Bodies*. Las Vegas: Central Recovery Press, 2017.

Mills, Charles W. *The Racial Contract*. Ithaca, NY: Cornell University Press, 1997.

Moore, Eddie, Ali Michael, and Marguerite W. Penick-Parks. *The Guide for White Women Who Teach Black Boys*. Thousand Oaks, CA: Corwin, 2017.

Moraga, Cherríe, and Gloria Andzaldúa, eds. *This Bridge Called My Back: Writings by Radical Women of Color*. New York: State University of New York Press, 2015.

Morrison, Toni. *Playing in the Dark: Whiteness and the Literary Imagination*. New York: Random House, 1992.

Oluo, Ijeoma. *So You Want to Talk About Race*. Berkeley, CA: Seal Press, 2018.

Raising Race Conscious Children. Home page. http://www.raceconscious.org.

Sensoy, Özlem, and Robin DiAngelo. *Is Everyone Really Equal? An Introduction to Key Concepts in Critical Social Justice Education*, 2nd ed. New York: Teachers College Press, 2017.

Shaheen, Jack G. "Reel Bad Arabs: How Hollywood Vilifies a People." *Annals of the American Academy of Political and Social Science* 588, no. 1 (2003).

Singleton, Glenn. *Courageous Conversations About Race: A Field Guide for Achieving Equity in Schools*. 2nd ed. Thousand Oaks, CA: Corwin, 2014.

Tatum, Beverly. *Why Are All the Black Kids Sitting Together in the Cafeteria: And Other Conversations About Race*, Twentieth anniv. rev. ed. New York: Basic Books, 2017.

Van Ausdale, Debra, and Joe R. Feagin. *The First R: How Children Learn Race and Racism*. Lanham, MD: Rowman & Littlefield, 2001.

Wise, Tim. *White Like Me: Reflections on Race from a Privileged Son*. Berkeley, CA: Soft Skull Press/Counterpoint, 2010.

FILMS

Chisholm '72: Unbought and Unbossed. Shola Lynch, dir. and prod. REAL-side, 2004. http://www.pbs.org/pov/chisholm.

A Class Divided. William Peters, dir. and prod. Yale University Films for *Frontline*, PBS. WGBH Education Foundation, 1985. https://www.pbs.org/wgbh/frontline/film/class-divided.

The Color of Fear. Stirfry Seminars, 1994. http://www.stirfryseminars.com/store/products/cof_bundle.php.

Cracking the Codes: The System of Racial Inequity. World Trust, 2013. https://world-trust.org.

Eyes on the Prize: America's Civil Rights Years 1954–1965. Season 1. DVD. Produced by Blackside for PBS, 2009. https://shop.pbs.org/eyes-on-the-prize-america-s-civil-rights-years-1954-1965-season-1-dvd/product/EYES600.

In Whose Honor? Jay Rosenstein, dir. On *POV* (PBS), premiered July 15, 1997. http://www.pbs.org/pov/inwhosehonor.

Mirrors of Privilege: Making Whiteness Visible. World Trust, 2007. https://world-trust.org.

Race: The Power of an Illusion. Larry Adelman, exec. prod. San Francisco: California Newsreel, 2003. http://www.pbs.org/race/000_General/000_00-Home.htm.

Reel Bad Arabs. Jeremy Earp, dir. Media Education Foundation, 2006. http://freedocumentaries.org/documentary/reel-bad-arabs.

The Revisionaries. Scott Thurman, dir. Making History Productions, 2012. http://www.pbs.org/independentlens/films/revisionaries.

13th. Ava DuVernay, dir. Netflix, 2016. https://www.netflix.com/title/80091741.

ACKNOWLEDGMENTS

I thank Idabelle Fosse, Reagen Price, Marxa Marnia, Christine Saxman, Shelly Tochluk, Aisha Hauser, Tee Williams, Dana Buhl, Kent Alexander, Sincere Kirabo, Malena Pinkham, Myosha McAfee, Resmaa Menakem, Devon Alexander, Darlene Flynn, Erin Trent-Johnson, Glen Singleton, Reverend John Crestwell, Özlem Sensoy, Deborah Terry, and Jason Toews for their invaluable contributions to various aspects of this work.

Thank you to the many people of color whose brilliance and patience has mentored me over the last twenty-five years. You understand white fragility and its roots in white identity far more than I ever will.

To my editor at Beacon Press, Rachael Marks, you were a dream to work with! My sincerest thanks for your perceptive feedback and encouragement.

NOTES

CHAPTER 1: THE CHALLENGES OF TALKING TO WHITE PEOPLE ABOUT RACISM

1. Angela Onwuachi-Willig, *According to Our Hearts: Rhinelander v. Rhinelander and the Law of the Multiracial Family* (New Haven, CT: Yale University Press, 2013).

2. Larry Adelman, *Race: The Power of an Illusion*, video (San Francisco: California Newsreel, 2003); Heather Beth Johnson and Thomas M. Shapiro, "Good Neighborhoods, Good Schools: Race and the 'Good Choices' of White Families," in *White Out: The Continuing Significance of Racism*, ed. Ashley W. Doane and Eduardo Bonilla-Silva (New York: Routledge, 2003), 173–87.

CHAPTER 2: RACISM AND WHITE SUPREMACY

1. Luigi Luca Cavalli-Sforza, Paolo Menozzi, and Alberto Piazza, *The History and Geography of Human Genes* (Princeton, NJ: Princeton University Press, 1994).

2. Richard S. Cooper, Jay S. Kaufman, and Ryk Ward, "Race and Genomics," *New England Journal of Medicine* 348, no. 12 (2003): 1166–70.

3. Resmaa Menakem, *My Grandmother's Hands: Racialized Trauma and the Pathway to Mending Our Hearts and Bodies* (Las Vegas: Central Recovery Press, 2017).

4. Thomas Jefferson, *Notes on the State of Virginia; with Related Documents*, ed. David Waldstreicher (Boston: Bedford/St. Martin's, 2002).

5. Nancy Leys Stepan and Sander L. Gilman, "Appropriating the Idioms of Science: The Rejection of Scientific Racism," in *The "Racial" Economy of Science: Toward a Democratic Future*, ed. Sandra Harding (Bloomington: Indiana University Press, 1993).

6. Ta-Nehisi Coates, *Between the World and Me* (New York: Spiegel & Grau, 2015).

7. Ibram X. Kendi, *Stamped from the Beginning* (New York: Nation Books, 2016).

8. Thomas F. Gossett, *Race: The History of an Idea* (New York: Oxford University Press, 1997); Noel Ignatiev, *How the Irish Became White* (New York: Routledge, 1995); Matthew Frye Jacobson, *Whiteness of a*

Different Color: European Immigrants and the Alchemy of Race (Cambridge, MA: Harvard University Press, 1999).

9. John Tehranian, "Performing Whiteness: Naturalization Litigation and the Construction of Racial Identity in America," *Yale Law Journal* 109, no. 4 (2000): 817–48.

10. Ignatiev, *How the Irish Became White*; Jacobson, *Whiteness of a Different Color*; David Roediger, *The Wages of Whiteness: Race and the Making of the American Working Class*, rev. ed. (1999; New York: Verso, 2003).

11. Roediger, *Wages of Whiteness*.

12. For an astute analysis of this "bargain" between working-class whites and owning-class whites, see Lillian Smith, *Killers of the Dream* (New York: W. W. Norton, 1949).

13. J. Kēhaulani Kauanui, "'A Structure, Not an Event': Settler Colonialism and Enduring Indigeneity," *Lateral: Journal of the Cultural Studies Association* 5, no. 1 (2016), https://doi.org/10.25158/L5.1.7.

14. Stuart Hall, *Representation: Cultural Representation and Signifying Practices* (London: Sage, 1997).

15. For a more detailed accounting of this documentation, see Robin DiAngelo, *What Does It Mean to Be White? Developing White Racial Literacy* (New York: Peter Lang, 2016).

16. Marilyn Frye, *The Politics of Reality: Essays in Feminist Theory* (Trumansburg, NY: Crossing Press, 1983).

17. David T. Wellman, *Portraits of White Racism* (Cambridge, UK: Cambridge University Press, 1977).

18. Peggy McIntosh, "White Privilege and Male Privilege: A Personal Account of Coming to See Correspondence Through Work in Women's Studies," in *Race, Class, and Gender: An Anthology*, ed. M. Anderson and P. Hill, 9th ed. (Belmont, CA: Wadsworth, 2012), 94–105.

19. Cheryl I. Harris, "Whiteness as Property," *Harvard Law Review* 106, no. 8 (1993): 1744.

20. George Lipsitz, *The Possessive Investment in Whiteness: How White People Profit from Identity Politics* (Philadelphia: Temple University Press, 2006), 1.

21. Ruth Frankenberg, "Local Whiteness, Localizing Whiteness," in *Displacing Whiteness: Essays in Social and Cultural Criticism*, ed. Ruth Frankenberg (Durham, NC: Duke University Press, 1997), 1.

22. Charles W. Mills, *The Racial Contract* (Ithaca, NY: Cornell University Press, 1997), 122.

23. Ibid., 1.

24. Ta-Nehisi Coates, "The Case for Reparations," *Atlantic*, June 2014, https://www.theatlantic.com/magazine/archive/2014/06/the-case-for-reparations/361631.

25. Mills, *The Racial Contract*, 40.

26. Haeyoun Park, Josh Keller, and Josh Williams, "The Faces of American Power, Nearly as White as the Oscar Nominees," *New York Times*, Feb-

ruary 26, 2016, https://www.nytimes.com/interactive/2016/02/26/us/race
-of-american-power.html; "All Time Box Office: Worldwide Grosses,"
Box Office Mojo, 2017, http://www.boxofficemojo.com/alltime/world/;
US Department of Education, Office of Planning, Evaluation and Policy
Development, Policy and Program Studies Service, *The State of Racial
Diversity in the Educator Workforce. Diversity* (Washington, DC: July
2016), https://www2.ed.gov/rschstat/eval/highered/racial-diversity/state
-racial-diversity-workforce.pdf; "Number of Full-Time Faculty Members
by Sex, Rank, and Racial and Ethnic Group, Fall 2007," *Chronicle of
Higher Education*, August 24, 2009, https://www.chronicle.com/article
/Numberof-Full-Time-Faculty/47992/.

27. Harrison Jacobs, "Former Neo-Nazi: Here's Why There's No Real Difference Between 'Alt-Right,' 'White Nationalism,' and 'White Supremacy,'"
Business Insider, August 23, 2017, http://www.businessinsider.com/why
-no-difference-alt-right-white-nationalism-white-supremacy-neo-nazi
-charlottesville-2017-8.

28. Derek Black, "'The Daily' Transcript: Interview with Former White Nationalist Derek Black," interview by Michael Barbaro, *New York Times*,
August 22, 2017, https://www.nytimes.com/2017/08/22/podcasts/the
-daily-transcript-derek-black.html.

29. Lee Atwater, interview with Alexander P. Lamis, July 8, 1981, quoted in
Alexander P. Lamis, *The Two-Party South* (New York: Oxford University
Press, 1984). The interviewee was originally described as an anonymous
insider; Atwater was not revealed as the person interviewed until the
1990 edition of the book. This interview was also quoted in Bob Herbert,
"Impossible, Ridiculous, Repugnant," *New York Times*, October 6, 2005.
Interpolations in original.

30. Joe R. Feagin, *The White Racial Frame: Centuries of Racial Framing and
Counter-Framing* (New York: Routledge, 2013).

31. Beverly Daniel Tatum, "Breaking the Silence," in *White Privilege: Essential Readings on the Other Side of Racism*, ed. Paula S. Rothenberg, 3rd
ed. (2001; New York: Worth Publishers, 2008), 147–52.

CHAPTER 3: RACISM AFTER THE CIVIL RIGHTS MOVEMENT

1. Martin Barker, *The New Racism: Conservatives and the Ideology of the
Tribe* (London: Junction Books, 1981).

2. Eduardo Bonilla-Silva, *Racism Without Racists: Color-Blind Racism and
the Persistence of Racial Inequality in America*, 4th ed. (2003; Lanham,
MD: Rowman & Littlefield, 2013).

3. Ibid.

4. John F. Dovidio, Peter Glick, and Laurie A. Rudman, eds., *On the Nature
of Prejudice: Fifty Years After Allport* (Malden, MA: Blackwell Publishing,
2005); Anthony G. Greenwald and Linda Hamilton Krieger, "Implicit Bias:
Scientific Foundations," *California Law Review* 94, no. 4 (2006): 945–67.

5. Marianne Bertrand and Sendhil Mullainathan, "Are Emily and Greg
More Employable Than Lakisha and Jamal? A Field Experiment on

Labor Market Discrimination," *American Economic Review* 94, no. 4 (September 2004): 991–1013.

6. Gordon Hodson, John Dovidio, and Samuel L. Gaertner, "The Aversive Form of Racism," *Psychology of Prejudice and Discrimination (Race and Ethnicity in Psychology)* 1 (2004): 119–36.

7. Lincoln Quillian and Devah Pager, "Black Neighbors, Higher Crime? The Role of Racial Stereotypes in Evaluations of Neighborhood Crime," *American Journal of Sociology* 107, no. 3 (November 2001): 717–67.

8. Toni Morrison, "On the Backs of Blacks," *Time*, December 2, 1993, http://content.time.com/time/magazine/article/0,9171,979736,00.html.

9. Robin DiAngelo, "The Sketch Factor: 'Bad Neighborhood' Narratives as Discursive Violence," in *The Assault on Communities of Color: Exploring the Realities of Race-Based Violence*, ed. Kenneth Fasching-Varner and Nicholas Daniel Hartlep (New York: Rowman & Littlefield, 2016).

10. Joe R. Feagin, *Systemic Racism: A Theory of Oppression* (New York: Taylor & Francis, 2006); Kristen Myers, "Reproducing White Supremacy Through Casual Discourse," in Doane and Bonilla-Silva, *White Out*, 129–44; Johnson and Shapiro, "Good Neighborhoods, Good Schools," 173–88; Robin DiAngelo and Özlem Sensoy, "Getting Slammed: White Depictions of Race Discussions as Arenas of Violence," *Race Ethnicity and Education* 17, no. 1 (2014): 103–28.

11. Kenneth B. Clark and Mamie P. Clark, "Emotional Factors in Racial Identification and Preference in Negro Children," *Journal of Negro Education* 19, no. 3 (1950): 341–50; Louise Derman-Sparks, Patricia G. Ramsey, and Julie Olsen Edwards, *What If All the Kids Are White? Anti-Bias Multicultural Education with Young Children and Families* (New York: Teachers College Press, 2006).

12. Jamelle Bouie, "Why Do Millennials Not Understand Racism?," Slate, May 16, 2014, http://www.slate.com/articles/news_and_politics/politics /2014/05/millennials_racism_and_mtv_poll_young_people_are_confused _about_bias_prejudice.html.

13. Leslie H. Picca and Joe R. Feagin, *Two-Faced Racism: Whites in the Backstage and Frontstage* (New York: Taylor and Francis, 2007).

14. Ibid.

CHAPTER 4: HOW DOES RACE SHAPE THE LIVES OF WHITE PEOPLE?

1. Carole Schroeder and Robin DiAngelo, "Addressing Whiteness in Nursing Education: The Sociopolitical Climate Project at the University of Washington School of Nursing," *Advances in Nursing Science* 33, no. 3 (2010): 244–55.

2. Melissah Yang, "Kinds of Shade," CNN.com, September 13, 2017, http://www.cnn.com/2017/09/13/entertainment/rihanna-fenty-beauty -foundation/index.html.

3. McIntosh, "White Privilege and Male Privilege."

4. Patrick Rosal, "To the Lady Who Mistook Me for the Help at the National Book Awards," *Literary Hub*, November 1, 2017, http://lithub .com/to-the-lady-who-mistook-me-for-the-help-at-the-national-book -awards.

5. McIntosh, "White Privilege and Male Privilege."

6. Ibid.

7. The compound closed in 2001 after having been bankrupted by litigation from the Southern Poverty Law Center.

8. McIntosh, "White Privilege and Male Privilege."

9. Sheila M. Eldred, "Is This the Perfect Face?," *Discovery News*, April 26, 2012.

10. Christine E. Sleeter, *Multicultural Education as Social Activism* (Albany, NY: SUNY Press, 1996), 149.

11. Unless otherwise noted, the information in this list comes from OXFAM, "An Economy for the 99%," briefing paper, January 2017, https://www .oxfam.org/en/research/economy-99.

12. Bloomberg Billionaire's Index, 2017, https://www.bloomberg.com /billionaires.

13. World Bank, *Annual GDP Rankings*, report, 2017, http://data.worldbank .org/data-catalog/GDP-ranking-table.

14. Bloomberg Billionaire's Index.

15. Matthew F. Delmont, *Why Busing Failed: Race, Media, and the National Resistance to School Desegregation* (Oakland: University of California Press, 2016).

16. Johnson and Shapiro, "Good Neighborhoods, Good Schools."

17. George S. Bridges and Sara Steen, "Racial Disparities in Official Assessments of Juvenile Offenders: Attributional Stereotypes as Mediating Mechanisms," *American Sociological Review* 63, no. 4 (1998): 554–70.

18. Kelly M. Hoffman, "Racial Bias in Pain Assessment and Treatment Recommendations, and False Beliefs About Biological Differences Between Blacks and Whites," *Proceedings of the National Academy of Science* 113, no. 16 (2016): 4296–4301.

19. Zeus Leonardo, "The Color of Supremacy: Beyond the Discourse of 'White Privilege,'" *Educational Philosophy and Theory* 36, no. 2 (2004): 137–52, published online January 9, 2013.

20. James Baldwin, response to Paul Weiss, *Dick Cavett Show*, 1965, video available at https://www.youtube.com/watch?v=_fZQQ7o16yQ.

21. Casey J. Dawkins, "Recent Evidence on the Continuing Causes of Black-White Residential Segregation," *Journal of Urban Affairs* 26, no. 3 (2004): 379–400; Johnson and Shapiro, "Good Neighborhoods, Good Schools."

22. Amy Stuart Wells, quoted in Nikole Hannah-Jones, "Choosing a School for My Daughter in a Segregated City," *New York Times Magazine*, June 9, 2016, https://www.nytimes.com/2016/06/12/magazine/choosing -a-school-for-my-daughter-in-a-segregated-city.html.

CHAPTER 5: THE GOOD/BAD BINARY

1. Barbara Trepagnier, *Silent Racism: How Well-Meaning White People Perpetuate the Racial Divide*, exp. ed. (orig. 2006; New York: Paradigm, 2010).
2. Omowale Akintunde, "White Racism, White Supremacy, White Privilege, and the Social Construction of Race: Moving from Modernist to Postmodernist Multiculturalism," *Multicultural Education* 7, no. 2 (1999): 1.
3. Derman-Sparks, Ramsey, and Edwards, *What If All the Kids Are White?*; Debra Van Ausdale and Joe R. Feagin, *The First R: How Children Learn Race and Racism* (Lanham, MD: Rowman & Littlefield, 2001).
4. Maria Benedicta Monteiro, Dalila Xavier de França, and Ricardo Rodrigues, "The Development of Intergroup Bias in Childhood: How Social Norms Can Shape Children's Racial Behaviors," *International Journal of Psychology* 44, no. 1 (2009): 29–39.
5. Van Ausdale and Feagin, *The First R*.

CHAPTER 6: ANTI-BLACKNESS

1. Frantz Fanon, *Black Skin, White Masks* (New York: Grove Press, 1952); Toni Morrison, *Playing in the Dark: Whiteness and the Literary Imagination* (New York: Random House, 1992).
2. Michelle Alexander, *The New Jim Crow: Mass Incarceration in the Age of Colorblindness* (New York: New Press, 2010); Bertrand and Mullainathan, "Are Emily and Greg More Employable than Lakisha and Jamal?"; Philip Oreopoulos and Diane Dechief, "Why Do Some Employers Prefer to Interview Matthew, but Not Samir? New Evidence from Toronto, Montreal, and Vancouver," working paper no. 95, Canadian Labour Market and Skills Researcher Network, February 2012, https://papers.ssrn.com/sol3/papers.cfm?abstract_id=2018047.
3. Susan E. Reed, *The Diversity Index: The Alarming Truth About Diversity in Corporate America . . . and What Can Be Done About It* (New York: AMACOM, 2011).
4. Alexander, *New Jim Crow*; Chauncee D. Smith, "Deconstructing the Pipeline: Evaluating School-to-Prison Pipeline Equal Protection Cases Through a Structural Racism Framework," *Fordham Urban Law Journal* 36 (2009): 1009; Pamela Fenning and Jennifer Rose, "Overrepresentation of African American Students in Exclusionary Discipline: The Role of School Policy," *Urban Education* 42, no. 6 (2007): 536–59; Sean Nicholson Crotty, Zachary Birchmeier, and David Valentine, "Exploring the Impact of School Discipline on Racial Disproportion in the Juvenile Justice System," *Social Science Quarterly* 90, no. 4 (2009): 1003–18; R. Patrick Solomon and Howard Palmer, "Black Boys Through the School-Prison Pipeline: When Racial Profiling and Zero Tolerance Collide," in *Inclusion in Urban Educational Environments: Addressing Issues of Diversity, Equity, and Social Justice*, ed. Denise E. Armstrong and Brenda J. McMahon (Charlotte, NC: Information Age Publishing, 2006), 191–212.

5. For the 7 percent cutoff and white flight, see Bonilla-Silva, *Racism Without Racists*. For declining housing demand, see Lincoln Quillian, "Why Is Black-White Residential Segregation So Persistent? Evidence on Three Theories from Migration Data," *Social Science Research* 31, no. 2 (2002): 197–229.

6. Coates, "The Case for Reparations."

7. Menakem, *My Grandmother's Hands*, 7.

8. Ta-Nehisi Coates, "The First White President: The Foundation of Donald Trump's Presidency Is the Negation of Barack Obama's Legacy," *Atlantic*, October 2017, https://www.theatlantic.com/magazine/archive/2017/10/the -first-white-president-ta-nehisi-coates/537909.

9. Sherene Razack, *Looking White People in the Eye: Gender, Race, and Culture in Courtrooms and Classrooms* (Toronto: University of Toronto Press, 1998).

10. Carol Anderson, *White Rage: The Unspoken Truth of Our Racial Divide* (New York: Bloomsbury, 2016).

11. The ideologies in this list are modified from a list in Özlem Sensoy and Robin DiAngelo, *Is Everyone Really Equal? An Introduction to Key Concepts in Critical Social Justice Education*, 2nd ed. (New York: Teachers College Press, 2017), 209.

CHAPTER 7: RACIAL TRIGGERS FOR WHITE PEOPLE

1. Michelle Fine, "Witnessing Whiteness," in *Off White: Readings on Race, Power, and Society*, ed. Michelle Fine, Lois Weis, Linda Powell Pruitt, and April Burns (New York: Routledge, 1997), 57.

2. Pierre Bourdieu, *The Field of Cultural Production: Essays on Art and Literature*, ed. Randal Johnson (New York: Columbia University Press, 1993).

3. Bourdieu termed these rules of each field's game "doxa."

4. Pierre Bourdieu, *Distinction: A Social Critique of the Judgement of Taste* (Cambridge, MA: Harvard University Press, 1984), 170.

5. Ibid.

CHAPTER 8: THE RESULT: WHITE FRAGILITY

1. Don Gonyea, "Majority of White Americans Say They Believe Whites Face Discrimination," NPR, October 24, 2017, https://www.npr.org /2017/10/24/559604836/majority-of-white-americans-think-theyre -discriminated-against.

2. Kenneth B. Clark, *Prejudice and Your Child* (Boston: Beacon Press, 1963); Derman-Sparks, Ramsey, and Edwards, *What If All the Kids Are White?*

3. Debian Marty, "White Antiracist Rhetoric as Apologia: Wendell Berry's *The Hidden Wound*," in *Whiteness: The Communication of Social Identity*, ed. Thomas Nakayama and Judith Martin (Thousand Oaks, CA: Sage, 1999), 51.

4. Ibid.; T. A. Van Dijk, "Discourse and the Denial of Racism," *Discourse and Society* 3, no. 1 (1992): 87–118.

5. DiAngelo and Sensoy, "Getting Slammed."
6. Morrison, *Playing in the Dark*.
7. Bonilla-Silva, *Racism Without Racists*, 68.
8. Rich Vodde, "De-Centering Privilege in Social Work Education: Whose Job Is It Anyway?," *Journal of Race, Gender and Class* 7, no. 4 (2001): 139–60.

CHAPTER 11: WHITE WOMEN'S TEARS

1. See, for example, Stacey Patton, "White Women, Please Don't Expect Me to Wipe Away Your Tears," *Dame*, December 15, 2014, http://www.damemagazine.com/2014/12/15/white-women-please-dont-expect-me-wipe-away-your-tears.
2. Ibid.

CHAPTER 12: WHERE DO WE GO FROM HERE?

1. Lorde, "The Uses of Anger."